PARADIGM SHIFTING

Guiding Evolution from the Inside

Paradigm Shifting:

Guiding Evolution from the Inside

By Jeff Carreira

Copyright © 2017

Emergence Education & Jeff Carreira

ISBN-10: 0-9969285-9-6

ISBN-13: 978-0-9969285-9-5

Library of Congress Control Number: 2017953226

Emergence Education Press

P.O. Box 63767, Philadelphia, PA 19147

www.EmergenceEducation.com

PARADIGM SHIFTING

Guiding Evolution from the Inside

JEFF CARREIRA

ACKNOWLEDGEMENTS

This book is dedicated to all of the many people
who support my work by caring about it…

…and all of the artists of possibility and articulators of
new paradigms who are currently finding and sharing their
unique voices…

….May you have the courage to speak it loudly

In addition I offer a special word of thanks to Jill Ouellette
for her invaluable editorial support

CONTENTS

Never doubt that a small group of thoughtful, committed individuals can change the world; indeed, it's the only thing that ever has.

Margaret Mead

It requires a very unusual mind to undertake the analysis of the obvious.

Alfred North Whitehead

It's not what you look at that matters, it's what you see.

Henry David Thoreau

"Tell me," Wittgenstein asked a friend, "why do people always say it was natural for man to assume that the sun went round the earth rather than that the earth was rotating?" His friend replied, "Well, obviously because it just looks as though the Sun is going round the Earth." Wittgenstein replied, "Well, what would it have looked like if it had looked as though the Earth was rotating?"

Ludwig Wittgenstein

INTRODUCTION

As you read this book please remember that it is not intended as an attempt to explain what reality is. In fact I don't think anyone knows what reality is and no one probably ever will. To go even further I believe that reality may not be anything in particular at all. Whatever it is that we call real is more fluid, flexible, and evanescent than we ever imagined.

We have been trained to think that we live in a universe full of stars and planets. And the stars and the planets and everything else are made of atoms and elements. We are taught that in this universe made of atoms some things are possible and others are not. I believe that reality is whatever universe of possibility we assume we live in, and that depends on what we believe in.

In this book you are invited to discover your truly co-creative power and the role that you already play in the ongoing creation of reality. You will learn about paradigms and how they are held together by ideas that we actively believe in without thinking to question. You will learn to question these foundational assumptions and dramatically expand your potential to transform.

This is an experiential journey. Reading these pages and engaging whole-heartedly with the thought experiments and exercises they contain will guide you through a process that will expand your awareness by unsettling the deeply unconscious assumptions that hold our current reality together.

Over twenty-five years ago I dedicated my life to seeking for answers to discover what was real, and what really mattered. What I've discovered so far can be summed up as follows.

We don't experience reality the way reality is. We experience reality the way we think it is. That means that what we experience as real is largely, and maybe entirely, a creation of mind.

You might think this discovery would be terrifying and yes, there is a part of us that only feels secure as long as our belief in the existence of a solid reality remains intact. But there is another part of us, the part that feels the limitations of the current paradigm. This part of us may have felt constrained by it for some time and might even have been trying to wriggle free. That part of us experiences elation at the discovery that reality is largely shaped by our mind because suddenly we don't know what's possible, and effectively that means that anything is.

Spiritual liberation is the experience of unlimited possibility, and that freedom brings us face to face with our awesome creative potential.

If our minds are generating our current experience of reality, then they should be able to create a new one.

Re-creating reality is what this book is ultimately about. We experience reality the way we do because we have been trained to experience it that way, not because it is that way. This book is a re-training for your mind.

With that in mind I encourage you to do more than read this book. Instead I would encourage you to work with it. Read slowly and think through each idea that is presented. I purposely wrote a short book using simple language to describe what are often complex and subtle concepts so you could grasp the ideas quickly and work with them.

At the end of each chapter you will find what I call a wormhole inquiry. Each of these inquiries offers a unique opportunity to look at the world differently.

Please give yourself some time to engage with the wormhole inquiries after you have already read and digested the chapter preceding it. When you engage with the inquiries, read through them two or three times to be sure you understand the instructions. Then give yourself twenty minutes at least to engage with them.

This book contains some of the most powerful contemplations I know of. The lines of inquiry I share here are the ones that have catalyzed big shifts in perspective for me. It is my sincere hope that they will do the same for you.

PART ONE
THE EVOLUTION OF SELF

In this section of the book we will explore the nature of what paradigms are, how profoundly we are embedded in them, and what makes it possible to shift them.

CHAPTER ONE
THE REALITY OF PARADIGM SHIFTING

This book is about our miraculous and essential capacity to create—and re-create—reality over and over again. It rests on the premise that reality is not something that is given from the start and etched in stone thereafter. It isn't "out there" forcing itself upon us. It isn't separate from us. We are part of it. It grows as we grow, and we grow as it grows.

We've been trained to assume that reality is the ever-present and unchanging background of life. In modern times science has become the arbiter of truth, and currently the truth that science shares with the public is that we live in a vast expanse of empty space filled with things. Some of those things are alive, and some of those living things have learned to think. We are the lucky ones because we are some of the ones who learned to think. We are thinking-things.

The things-in-space universe and the thinking-thing model of human life are the two most foundational pillars of the paradigm that we currently live in. This book was written for those individuals who are at least starting to feel suffocated by the limitations of the current paradigm. You may be utterly convinced, or you might just have a hunch, but somehow or other you've started to seriously question the ultimate validity of limiting your existence to being a thinking-thing. This kind of questioning of our own existence is a time-honored path to spiritual freedom that has been known to release profound capacities for wisdom and love.

Attaining spiritual freedom has been the obsession of my life, and this book is the result of decades of spiritual pursuit and the fruits I have been graced with. Those years of spiritual practice and experience have led me to the conviction that the value of spirituality at this moment in human history is to awaken our capacities to paradigm shift. We see ourselves in a world suffering from global challenges that we don't seem able to avert. Many people are aware that the future of our species and maybe our planet depend on the emergence of a new paradigm that will dramatically shift human consciousness. The things-in-space/thinking-thing worldview has only been the Western paradigm for a few hundred years. Before then we lived in the God-centered world of the Middle Ages. That universe was a strange place where the earth was flat and surrounded by a set of perforated spheres that allowed the light of heaven to shine through. The stars we see at night were not burning gaseous clouds; they were holes in the heavenly spheres.

Paradigms have consequences. The paradigm of the Middle Ages allowed for only certain ways for humans to live. The Renaissance and the Enlightenment ushered in the things-in-space/thinking-thing paradigm that we currently live in. That paradigm shift dramatically altered human life. Now we find ourselves at the faltering edge of that paradigm where it no longer seems capable of addressing the needs of our species or our planet. We need a shift in paradigm—or perhaps we need to accelerate a shift that started a long time ago.

As I said, this book was written to support those who are actively working to facilitate a shift in paradigm for humanity. I like to call such people *articulators of new paradigms* or *artists of possibility*. These phrases describe the work of paradigm shifting. That work involves opening ourselves to an alternative vision of reality and then expressing that vision to others so that the energy of it spreads into existence. This book is my articulation of some of my deepest recognitions of a new reality, along with my thoughts about the activity of paradigm shifting.

I believe the key lies in our deep spiritual yearnings. Our desire for spiritual release and liberation is part of a universal awakening that we are being called to participate in. I don't believe that we live in a universe of empty space. It makes much more sense to me that we are part of a universe that is a vast, living, intelligent being that is becoming more conscious all the time. The universe is waking up, and our awakening is part of its awakening. Our desire to awaken beyond the limits of separation and find our true place as part of a larger wholeness is how we experience the universe's desire to realize its full potential.

We are currently confined within a separate sense of self that cannot hold the totality of who we are and what we are capable of. That limited self-image has reached its intellectual, emotional, and perceptual limits, and many of us realize that we must expand this limited self in order to create the future we see in our most inspired moments. The first step in this profound process of growth is the release of our spirit from its uncomfortably tight orbit around our ego. This is what spiritual freedom is.

In these opening paragraphs I have been describing spiritual freedom from the vantage point of the separate sense of self. Looking at the quest for spiritual freedom as part of a universal awakening is more difficult. In this book you will see that from the universe's point of view the ultimate spiritual bondage is our unquestioned belief in our own existence. The fact that we think that we are someone that could become spiritually liberated is one of the beliefs that the greater being of the universe is attempting to wriggle itself free from.

When I talk about the greater being of the universe, I am not talking about a physical being. I am referring to an intelligent and sensitive energy that is the life force running through all of manifestation. This life-force energy is the living source that animates the entire world, including our own minds and bodies. It is our spirit, and it is ready to expand beyond our current human form if we allow it to. So from the universe's point of view spiritual liberation means the liberation of the life-force energy from the constraints of our current human self-concept.

The universal energy that moves through us is funneled through the beliefs we hold about ourselves and the world. That mysterious energy is capable of much more than we can currently imagine, and so as we release ourselves from the belief systems and paradigms we are currently bound up in, we simultaneously allow the creative energy of the universe to find new expressions for its own manifestation. This is how a new reality is born—not just a new human reality—but a reality beyond what we can currently conceptualize.

This book is an inquiry into what a paradigm actually is, how it works to keep us locked inside, and how new paradigms can be born. We have a journey ahead of us to make all of this intellectually and experientially clear, and I hope you will stay with me to the very last page.

Throughout this book we will return again and again to the one key insight that makes paradigm shifting possible. That insight is this: our perception is filtered and shaped by a paradigm, and when we inquire into the nature of that paradigm, that inquiry is itself shaped by the paradigm we are questioning.

What makes this kind of investigation so tricky is that we are looking at something that is shaping how we look. As you read through the explorations and inquiries in these pages, please remember that the part of you that is reading is also being shaped by the same mechanisms that you are reading about. If this sounds like an impossible trap, it isn't, and in this book you'll learn how the subtle territory of paradigm shifting can be navigated so that you can *use the mind to go beyond the mind,* as the expression goes. In the end, it is my sincere hope that you will open to a dramatically altered experience of reality.

Let's start this journey by exploring just how deeply and inextricably shaped we actually are by the paradigms we currently live in.

Paradigms affect who we are at many levels. Some are more familiar to us while others lie buried in our unconsciousness. Let's start with a familiar experience that we can all relate to, namely, the fact that we all occasionally get stuck in a rut. By this I mean that we get caught in rigid beliefs and conclusions that shape our experience and how we show up in the world.

How many people are working in jobs and careers they detest because they're trapped inside the belief that they can't afford to leave? How many people avoid doing new things out of fear of one kind or another? How many people do things they shouldn't because they believe they can't stop? There are so many ways that we get stuck in ideas—some of them serve us for the better, others don't.

In a psychological context this kind of shaping is often referred to as conditioning. We are all conditioned to see ourselves and the world in particular ways. A simple definition of a paradigm would be: the entire collection of thoughts and feelings that condition us into having the experience we're having right now.

There are superficial layers of conditioning made up of the personal ruts that catch us in conclusions based on our personal experience. Imagine someone who was once embarrassed by a grade school teacher for misspelling a word and then concluded they couldn't spell. Because "they knew" they "couldn't spell" they tended not to even try and were always quick to ask others for the correct spelling of every word. You can probably imagine how this behavior over years would in fact make spelling difficult for them. A conclusion they drew about themselves had become a rut that shaped the reality of who they were.

Now, if for some reason that person were to change that conclusion and suddenly believe that they could spell, their behavior would change as well. They would start to try to spell things out, and learning from their mistakes they would gradually become a good speller. In this small way a shift in paradigm led to personal transformation.

Traditional psychotherapy is often aimed at supporting this kind of paradigm shift. All too often we internalize profoundly negative beliefs about ourselves, other people, or life in general based on traumatic experiences. Psychotherapy can help bring these beliefs into awareness to be questioned so that the original conclusion can be released and more accurate and healthy conclusions adopted.

These personal layers of conditioning are the most superficial and the easiest to transcend. At deeper levels we find that we have adopted whole sets of cultural beliefs and predispositions that shape us. These cultural beliefs typically remain unconscious to us—unless of course we have the opportunity to spend time in a different culture, where they can become blindingly obvious.

Our nationality, for instance, shapes us in many ways. Americans tend to express themselves differently from Europeans and both differently from people living in Asian cultures. Men are conditioned to experience and act differently than women are. Older people have developed different habits of mind and action than younger people.

Professions and work environments also come with value systems attached to them, and these condition the practitioners of particular fields and the people working in certain environments. Even as part of a circle of friends we condition each other in different ways.

If we go deeper than this, we find that there are beliefs about what it means to be human that cross over cultural boundaries. Today many of these supra-cultural beliefs come to us through the theories of modern science. Science in today's world has become the source of a meta-narrative about what is real and what is not that generates some of the most profound and stubborn sources of conditioning that shape us.

Part of what I want to do in this book is show how for those of us in the West—and increasingly throughout the world—many of our scientific conclusions about reality need to be questioned. Not because science is wrong necessarily, but because there are ways of understanding reality that lie outside of science's purview that need deeper consideration. In addition, the science that shapes our common understanding of reality is not the most current science. In fact most of our mental models of reality are drawn from scientific ideas that are hundreds of years old. An entirely new scientific paradigm has emerged over the past century that is yet to be incorporated into our current worldview.

We cannot consider the influence of science on the modern paradigm without discussing the book that introduced the idea of paradigm shifting into the popular lexicon. *The Structure of Scientific Revolutions* by the historian of science Thomas Kuhn was one of the most influential American publications of the twentieth century. In it Kuhn shows how the true history of science is punctuated by periodic paradigm shifts that radically alter the foundational assumptions that all of science had previously rested on. The science that is practiced after a paradigm shift is a different kind of science than what was practiced before.

Two foundational assumptions of the modern scientific paradigm are materialism and reductionism. Materialism is the assumption that reality is ultimately made of matter—physical stuff—and that life and consciousness are by-products of material processes. Reductionism is the belief that everything is made up of parts and that you can understand everything by understanding the parts that it is made of. This book will challenge both of these assumptions by offering new and existing ways to think about and perceive the world around you. As you feel your way into a universe that begins with consciousness and where parts are reflections of wholes, you will experience the exuberant realization that everything can change.

The scientific paradigm is a very deep source of our conditioning, but there are deeper layers of conditioned beliefs that exist even below this. Underneath the relatively recent conclusions of science there are earlier religious and philosophical assumptions about ourselves that form the ground that even our scientific paradigm stands on.

In this book we will question the idea that we are entities that live in the world. Right now you and me and everyone else are having the experience of being someone in the world. We experience ourselves as a person who experiences a world that exists outside of us. Where did that idea come from? When did we decide that we were separate from the world?

This division of self and world is most often attributed to the French philosopher René Descartes, who solidified the idea that human beings have an inside world of thought and feeling that is separate from the outside world of bodies and objects. He divided reality into subjects—things that experience—and objects—things that are experienced. This fundamental division is one of the most profound shaping influences of the paradigm we currently live in. We could call it the paradigm of separation in large part because it is built on an assumption that we are subjects who experience objects that are separate from us.

If you look around, you will see quite easily that you experience yourself as a thing that experiences other things. And you assume that your experience of those other things is happening inside your mind. When you begin to question an assumption this deep, you notice something interesting. It's hard to even imagine another possibility because the act of asking the question already feels like it is happening in your subjective experience. When we ask a question this deep, we get into the territory we mentioned earlier where we have to find a way to compensate for the fact that the question we are asking is already being shaped by the paradigm element that we are attempting to question.

This depth of inquiry is where our work together in this book will focus. Of course profound transformations can come from shifting more superficial personal and cultural paradigms, but if we overturn our current scientific and philosophical belief systems, the amount of change that will be ushered in is unimaginable.

There is one more thing that I would like to do before we bring this first chapter to a close. I want to take everything that we have discussed so far and propose a model of reality that might replace the one we have learned. This model will outline how the sense of self developed out of layers of conclusions about reality that emerged out of a field of pure consciousness.

As a starting point for this model, I look towards the time-honored mystical and esoteric traditions of the East and West that recognize the foundation of life to be an all-knowing consciousness. Some traditions refer to this omnipresent awareness as God, others as the Self, and others as the Absolute. We will start our model of reality by similarly assuming that the ultimate source of reality is a primary conscious unity or Oneness.

In this book we will also assume that we can have a direct personal awareness of this source that we will call an experience of pure awareness or non-duality. Pure awareness is just awareness without being aware of anything and without knowing that it is aware. Because it sees nothing outside of itself, it also recognizes no distinctions—no self, no other, no this, no that, no now, no then—no difference and no separation. It is the consciousness of Unity. It is pure awareness without an object. It sees everything but is blind to everything that it sees. It is wild and free because it has not yet been shaped by any ideas, beliefs, or notions.

The nineteenth century American philosopher Charles Sanders Peirce spent his life working out a model of reality starting with exactly this kind of pure awareness. He called it "firstness" because it existed first, before anything else. The passage below, taken from one of his essays, is my personal favorite description of non-dual consciousness.

The idea of the absolutely First must be entirely separated from all conception of or reference to anything else; for what involves a second is itself a second to that second. The First must therefore be present and immediate, so as not to be second to a representation. It must be fresh and new, for if old it is second to its former state. It must be initiative, original, spontaneous, and free; otherwise it is second to a determining cause. It is also something vivid and conscious; so only it avoids being the object of some sensation. It precedes all synthesis and all differentiation; it has no unity and no parts. It cannot be articulately thought: assert it, and it has already lost its characteristic innocence; for assertion always implies a denial of something else. Stop to think of it, and it has flown! What the world was to Adam on the day he opened his eyes to it, before he had drawn any distinctions, or had become conscious of his own existence—that is first, present, immediate, fresh, new, initiative, original, spontaneous, free, vivid, conscious, and evanescent. Only, remember that every description of it must be false to it.

Peirce's description of the original source of reality gives us a visceral sense of the Oneness of non-dual pure awareness. In the model that I am proposing the starting point of reality is this pure consciousness before any objects had appeared in reality that could be seen and prior to the formation of any sense of identity that could see. In this awareness nothing has happened, and anything is possible. It is the deepest core of who we all are because at that depth of being we are That. My wording here reflects my background in the Hindu tradition of Advaita Vedanta, in which the phrase "I am That" was immortalized by the Indian sage Nisargadatta Maharaj, but as I said earlier, you can find analogous conceptions in most of the world's great spiritual traditions.

Pure awareness is free because it has not yet been shaped by anything. It has not been captivated by any paradigm or belief system whatsoever. How could it be when there are no identifiable thoughts yet to get caught in?

Now imagine that in this field of pure awareness a process of conceptualization and identification got started that ultimately created the solid sense of self and rigid experience of the world that we currently live in.

Over time layers of identification formed in the initial Unity. First an experience appeared, and then an idea about that experience followed. Then another experience occurred followed by more ideas. The experiences and the ideas about them that followed became more complex until we ended up where we are now—having an experience of being the person that we are, living in the world we've become familiar with.

It is only the very first chapter, and I realize I've already presented you with a model of reality that is dramatically different than the models we were taught in school. I am not talking about a Big Bang of light, heat, and atoms. There is no formation of elements like hydrogen, helium, and carbon. There is no cooling of galaxies, stars, and planets. Nor is there an emergence of life or an evolution of species. I have presented for your consideration a model of the growth of reality that starts with consciousness and describes the development of conscious experience rather than physical elements. I am offering a cosmology of consciousness to consider in place of the more familiar conception of the evolution of the physical universe.

The alternative universe story that I propose is based on the conviction that the reality we experience has been generated by a process of successively layered conceptualizations rather than from the energetic interactions of tiny physical particles. It poses a direct challenge to our materialistic viewpoint. Of course, I am not alone in believing that we need to reconsider our materialistic and reductionistic view of reality; in fact, Dr. Robert Lanza, whose theory of biocentrism makes this exact point, was named one of the most influential people of 2014. So there are voices speaking about this at the edges of acceptable science. (Although Lanza was named one of Time magazine's most influential people his concept of Biocentrism is still controversial in the scientific community.) I realize this model may be difficult to understand at this early stage from this brief description, but I promise if you continue on the journey of this book it will make more and more sense to you by the end.

In the model that we are developing here each next layer of conceptualization shapes what is real and therefore what is possible in particular ways. Eventually the ideas about a self form, and each new idea limits the self by making it more particular. As layer after layer of conceptualization form, the self becomes distinct and increasingly differentiated from everything else.

The outer layers of identification are made up of obvious beliefs that we hold about ourselves; for example, I am a writer, I am a friend, I am good at public speaking, I can't spell, etc. Below these are the layers of cultural identification. The first few ideas that make up the core of our identity are beliefs like "I think" and "I am alive," and perhaps closest to the source is simply the idea "I am." Below the level of "I am" there is only "isness," that pure being that cannot hold any ideas about itself. That is the non-dual conscious source of awareness.

Many spiritual traditions envision the path to enlightenment or God-realization as the gradual or sudden shedding of all of these layers of identification, leading ultimately to an experience of non-duality or God-realization in which we become one with our source. In some traditions the ultimate spiritual goal is described as permanent abidance in that pure awareness.

Here we will explore how the experience of non-duality gives rise to a tremendous opportunity for existential creativity. Once we shed the layers of identification that separate us from our source, we can deliberately re-identify with new ideas and new ways of thinking and re-create ourselves and the world.

The ideas and inquiries that are presented in this book are designed to loosen the layers of identification that are holding us and the world in their familiar state. At the same time they provide new possibilities to explore. In the next few chapters I will explain a method of inquiry that can change everything. I call it wormhole inquiry.

WORMHOLE INQUIRY

At the end of each chapter I will offer a wormhole inquiry like the following that will allow you to operationalize the understanding of the chapter. I will explain my thinking behind the idea of wormhole inquiries in the next chapter. In the meantime, you can experiment with this one. Doing these mental exercises will expand this work beyond the intellectual so that you can experientially explore these new ideas.

In this chapter we explored how we are shaped by the limiting beliefs and false conclusions that we have drawn about ourselves over time. It is likely that the vast majority of these are unconscious, but there are usually some that we know about.

In this first wormhole inquiry I ask you to identify a limiting belief or false notion that shapes your behavior in some negative way. "I'm not good at making money," "I'm too shy to meet people," or "I'm not talented enough to sing on stage" are a few examples.

Once you have a limiting belief in mind, write it out on paper. Think about how this belief shapes you in different circumstances and how you might show up differently in those circumstances without it.

The next time you enter into one of the circumstances in which you know you are shaped by this false idea, simply change the way you show up. Act as if you didn't have that idea about yourself and see what happens.

It will be difficult; you will probably feel awkward; but do it anyway. What you will notice is that part of what makes it uncomfortable is that you feel like you are faking. You feel like the way you usually are is true and this is pretense. Why is it that we believe the false ideas we've held about ourselves for a long time are more accurate than the alternative?

If you spend more time acting in opposition to your negative false beliefs about yourself, something amazing will start to happen. You will start to feel more comfortable being different, and this will make you seriously question the validity of the original belief.

Maybe that original belief feels more like you because you've acted out of it for so long. If you act differently and that starts to feel like you, what does that mean about who you are?

CHAPTER TWO
THE ART OF WORMHOLE INQUIRY

What I am calling wormhole inquiries are philosophical hacks that free us from strict adherence to our current belief system and propel us into the open-ended possibility field of the unknown. You could think of them as modern day Zen koans—riddles so powerful that the mere contemplation of them can blow your mind and catapult you into a new world.

The inquiries you find in this book have been carefully designed to challenge some of the most foundational assumptions upon which your entire worldview rests. These assumptions are so deeply embedded in your psyche that you don't generally see them at all. They are simply part of the invisible background that allows you to make sense of the world and everything in it. Without them you may find yourself feeling adrift with no reference points upon which to create meaning. This may be a little scary, but if you recognize it as part of the process of shifting out of one paradigm and into another, you will also find it thrilling.

Questioning our foundational assumptions and bringing them into the light of conscious contemplation thrusts us into a profound state of uncertainty. Challenging even a few of the pillars that our current conception of reality rests upon inevitably forces us to question everything we think is real. I see this as a transformational use of philosophy, and it is an essential practice for those of us who want to do everything we can to facilitate the massive shift in paradigm that many people believe our world needs.

Philosophy is generally thought of as a means of determining what is true, but when philosophy is used as a means of determining truth it can't help but be mired in the currently dominant paradigm. You see, the fact that there is a truth that could be known and understood rationally by the mind is a very recent development in Western culture and a pillar of the current paradigm. The modern world that we are familiar with was born in the era known as the Enlightenment, which rests squarely on the insight that human beings are creatures with minds capable of understanding the mysteries of the natural world. This may not seem like a particularly novel idea to you, but a few hundred years ago it was a truly revolutionary notion.

Before the Enlightenment it was assumed that only God had the power of mind capable of understanding anything. In fact, early Enlightenment thinkers were often burned at the stake or imprisoned and tortured for having the hubris to think they could know something. It was dangerous to speak as if you could understand anything.

In the modern scientific paradigm the tables have turned—we are no longer afraid to know; what terrifies us today is the insecurity of not knowing. I believe our future depends on discovering the freedom of mind that can only be found by embracing the uncertainty of not knowing wholeheartedly. Thinking we can know things definitively has become dangerous because reality is simply too mysterious, too complex, too vast, and too multi-dimensional to ever be fully understood.

As I have come to experience more and more of the deeper mysteries of life, I find myself increasingly uneasy with fixed ideas and final conclusions. Of course, I still want to know concrete things like how to earn money, get from place to place, and be a good friend, but when I start to feel too settled in my existential beliefs about reality I find myself feeling uncomfortable. Strict adherence to any set of existential beliefs about the way things are makes me feel boxed in and vulnerable, and I quickly want to challenge my own positions with new ideas to make sure I am not stuck in an existential rut.

In the current paradigm, we've been conditioned to feel uncomfortable with not knowing. As soon as we realize that there is something we do not know, we immediately feel compelled to try to understand it. In and of itself this wouldn't be so bad except that too often our efforts to understand are only motivated by our desire to feel secure. Once we are convinced that we know something, we no longer feel compelled to think about it. We simply go on our way. In the worse-case scenario we will defend our ignorance rather than face the insecurity of not knowing.

What this ultimately means is that our inquiries generally focus exclusively on what we think we don't know, leaving those things that we feel certain about largely unexamined. In this book you will discover that the most powerful contemplations occur when we focus on what we feel most certain about. Our investigations into what seems most obviously true are precisely the ones that can release us from the limitations of the current paradigm. In the end we need to uproot and examine our most settled beliefs about reality because those are the ones holding the entire paradigm together.

Uprooting and examining our existential convictions is challenging because we haven't been trained to use our minds this way. We have been trained to replace not-knowing with knowing, but the wormhole inquiries you engage with in this book will take you in the opposite direction—from knowing to not knowing. With focused and sustained effort we can uproot our current belief system through deep consideration of viable alternatives. In doing this, our natural inclination will be to want to settle on the new alternative, but that will only move us from one belief system to another.

The philosophical inquiry that I am advocating is not designed to give us a new understanding of reality. Its aim is to leave us deeply uncertain about what is real. To a modern mind this might feel frightening and dangerous, but that's only because the modern mind is founded on the belief that not knowing is dangerous and we *should* be able to know and understand everything. I believe just the opposite is true.

The experience of knowing leaves us satisfied and confident. We stop thinking and examining. The experience of not knowing makes us uncomfortable and compels us to question. When we don't know, we become open and receptive and actively engaged in a quest for answers. This position of uncertainty is the one we need to adopt and become comfortable with if we want to navigate unendingly through the mysteries of life.

If you think about it for a moment, it makes perfect sense. When we want to know something, like how to get to the store, we feel comfortable as long as we have clear directions in our head. If we are driving off to the store without knowing where it is, we should feel uncomfortable because just driving around hoping to find the store is probably not going to work. But when it comes to existential questions about what is real and what gives life meaning, we are often much better served by the open stance of not knowing.

What I am saying was well known to Charles Sanders Peirce, whom I quoted in the last chapter and whose ideas we will visit periodically in the chapters ahead. Peirce was one of the originators of the American philosophy of pragmatism, and he lived according to the motto, "Never block the road to inquiry." And, of course, thinking that you already know is one of the surest ways to block the road of inquiry. At the heart of Peirce's philosophy was what he called the doctrine of fallibilism, which simply states that any of our current beliefs, no matter how certain we may feel about them, might be wrong and almost certainly will be found to be wrong eventually.

How could it be otherwise?

Here we are living on a single planet revolving around a single star in a galaxy that contains trillions of stars. We are smaller than a speck in our galaxy, and our galaxy is itself only one of trillions of galaxies in the universe.

We have access to the conscious understanding of only one biological form, and we have knowledge of a mere few thousand years of our own history.

We know that our eyes only see a tiny fragment of the electro-magnetic spectrum, and our ears only hear a tiny amount of the sound around us. In short, we don't have any way of knowing how minuscule a portion of the universe we actually have access to through our senses, but it seems likely that we are aware of only a tiny portion of all possible knowledge in the universe.

In short we only know what we know, and there is no way to know how small a sample of the whole that is. And that is only in relationship to what can be known. We couldn't even begin to fathom how much more reality there might be in the universe that is unknowable to us in our current form. Thinking this way makes any assumption we have that we already know the way reality works seem dramatically presumptuous. Of course, at the same time, the belief that we don't know how reality works is itself just another belief that might be wrong.

The question is, who among us has the courage to live in the unknown? Because those that do will be available to question our most cherished and foundational beliefs by posing viable alternatives—not to adopt as new beliefs, but to continually shake us out of complacency and open us into new possibilities to be explored and lived. Those of us willing to venture beyond the edges of the known become artists of possibility and articulators of new paradigms. We become transitional beings continually serving further growth by breaking away old ideas the way icebreaking ships break up floating ice on the sea, keeping the waterways open and allowing other ships safe passage.

As you engage in your own wormhole inquiries throughout your reading of this book, please avoid the temptation to latch on to each new idea and get stuck there. Allow a new way of understanding to rest in juxtaposition against more culturally accepted views. The magic is not in the new idea. It is in the friction between competing explanations of reality. The discomfort that appears between equally viable alternative explanations creates a wormhole that you just might fall through into an expanse of pure possibility. The unlimited freedom of this expanse may feel frightening at first, but if you can avoid the almost overwhelming temptation to seek security by latching on to the next idea, you can enter into a life of ongoing revelation that is nothing less than miraculous.

As I mentioned in chapter one, many years ago I dedicated myself to the pursuit of spiritual awakening. I left the life I had been living and embarked on an adventure without any map of the territory. For decades I lived a life that gave me the time and space to do as much spiritual practice and philosophical contemplation as anyone could ever want.

Over all those years I was blessed with more breakthrough experiences and energetic openings than I can remember. Some were dramatic; others were so subtle that they could almost be missed; but what they all have in common is that they instantaneously shifted my perspective and brought me into a new perception of reality.

When we call an experience spiritual, mystical, or transformative, this is often the quality we are speaking of. These experiences are life altering because they do more than just illuminate the world as it is—they reveal new worlds of possibility to us.

When we experience these reality-shifting moments, it's like falling through a wormhole. A wormhole is a cosmological term. It is hypothesized that there are warps in space and time that immediately connect distant points in the universe. Theoretically, if we were to travel through one end of a wormhole, we would instantaneously find ourselves in a distant part of the universe.

Many of my most profound spiritual experiences feel like this. One minute I'm meditating or contemplating or just walking outside, and suddenly something happens—an experience, an insight, or just a shift—and the world has changed and everything is different.

The journeys through spiritual wormholes that I have been blessed with have taught me that there are certain practices that seem to hold our attention near the edge of a potential wormhole. When we engage in these practices, we are effectively dancing at the very edge of a shift in perception in the hopes of falling over. If we dance there long enough, it is inevitable that we will eventually find ourselves in another world of possibility.

There are forms of contemplation and inquiry that offer equally powerful opportunities to dance on the edges of wormholes. Whenever we question our foundational assumptions about life, ourselves, or the nature of reality as we know it, we start inching our way right up to the edge of the known universe. If we keep asking questions, we start leaning over the edge, and eventually we will topple over.

Zen masters have used the spiritual art of the koan for thousands of years to provoke dramatic shifts in awareness. Koans are questions that at first glance appear to be nonsensical. Perhaps the most famous Zen koan is the question, "What is the sound of one hand clapping?"

The great Indian sage Ramana Maharshi famously asked his disciples to use the simple question, "Who am I?" as what I see as a wormhole inquiry. During the decades that he lived and taught, he guided thousands of his followers into radical states of realization using this simple question. I spent many years working in the lineage of Ramana, and you may notice that many of the wormhole inquiries I suggest in this book are variations of his instruction.

In general, when I teach philosophy, I use simple and penetrating questions to challenge foundational assumptions of our current reality. Some of the questions I am particularly fond of are:

Does thinking happen inside of us?

Am I really separate from you?

Is yesterday really gone?

Is tomorrow already here?

These are the kinds of questions that can take us into an instantaneous shift in consciousness and perspective. They are great worm-holing questions.

Today philosophy is too often thought of as a merely academic endeavor involving reading, understanding, and commenting on texts. When I use the word *philosophy*, I am referring to the art of questioning our most fundamental assumptions about reality and then courageously following those questions until a new world of possibility opens up before our very eyes. This is the art of wormhole inquiry.

WORMHOLE INQUIRY

If our goal is paradigm shifting, the most important thing for us to learn is how to question the validity of those things that we feel most certain about already.

One of the things that we feel most unquestionably certain about is our own existence. In this book you will be asked to question the validity of your belief in your own existence. In this wormhole inquiry I want you to ask yourself the question, "Who am I?" repeatedly.

Who are you? What is it that responds when your name is called? What is it that answers the questions that are directed at you?

When you contemplate this simple question, you quickly realize that every answer that you come up with is not who you are. They are all aspects of who you are, characteristics of you, but they are not you. You are always the one who has those characteristics.

Who is it that all of the characteristics are connected to?

If you stay with this question long enough, all you will see is a swirl of characteristics. Ideas about who you are, what you do, how you feel, etc. None of these are you.

What will begin to open up is a mystery. Somehow all of these accumulated ideas have gathered like a cloud. You have always assumed that you existed somewhere in the middle of that cloud, but now you're not so sure.

Maybe there is nothing in the middle that all the characteristics are connected to. Maybe you don't exist in the way that you always thought you did.

If you are able to follow this inquiry into this mysterious place, just rest there. Be with the emptiness and the mystery that you are without trying to make something out of it. Feel the freedom of not knowing if you exist. If you don't know that you exist, you could be anything, including nothing at all.

CHAPTER THREE
RESTING BETWEEN WORLDS

In the last chapter we began our exploration of worm-holing and created a context for how it works and why it is important. This chapter will further that exploration with a description of what it feels like to enter into a paradigm-shifting wormhole.

At the start it is important to realize that our minds have been trained in a very particular form of thinking. We haven't just been taught to think; we've been taught how to think, which includes learning a particular way of understanding what a mind is and how it works. We have been taught that a mind is a storehouse for the knowledge and information that we accumulate through our senses and that it is a calculating machine that uses information to generate pictures and stories that explain the world and allow us to solve problems.

This representational theory of mind sees our conscious experience as a mirror of reality and assumes that we see things objectively. We have learned that knowledge about the world is different from opinions about it. In other words we feel certain that it is possible to use our minds to find a detached vantage point so that we can understand the way things *really* are. To put it bluntly, we have been taught that there is a right way to see everything and that we can use the pictures and stories in our heads to figure out what it is.

The assumption that there is one right truth and that it can only be discovered from a detached point of view is an important one to challenge because it is another source of separation in the paradigm of separation. If we believe that reality is what's left when our opinions have been separated out of our experience, then we have effectively decided that we are somehow separate from reality. So we will have to question our ideas about objective truth to discover a way of thinking about reality that won't separate us from it.

In addition, the firm belief that there is only one right way to understand truth doesn't leave much room for a different possibility. We are effectively locking ourselves into reality exactly as it is without leaving the opportunity of discovering an alternative. We have been trained that reality just is what it is and there is nothing much we can do to change it. Yes, we might be able to alter some aspects of reality, but we won't be able to fundamentally change reality itself. Paradigm shifting, on the other hand, means changing reality, not just changing aspects of reality, and so to engage with it we have to question our assumptions about what reality is.

In the inquiries in this book we will assume that our understanding of the world is never separate from the world. Reality is not something separate from me that exists prior to my pictures and stories about it. The pictures and stories I create to understand reality are part of reality. I am continuously engaged in a participatory process that endlessly co-creates what is.

One of the foundational insights that everything in this book rests on is that reality isn't just sitting there waiting for us to make pictures of and tell stories about. Reality comes into existence as we create pictures and tell stories about it. In short, our understanding of reality is part of reality. By following the inquiries in this book you will begin to understand how this happens and how we can more consciously participate in the creation of the future.

This is not the way we've been trained to see things. We've been trained to assume that reality exists independent of us, and we develop an understanding of it that lives in our head. Think about your childhood cartoons. How often did you see a trail of thought bubbles drifting away from someone's head and in the biggest bubble an image that mirrored the scene around them?

These seemingly innocuous cartoons are narrating a cultural story that defines our age. The story is that you are an entity with the cognitive capacity to generate an image in your head of the reality around you. As you get older, the story gets more sophisticated, and you learn that you have a brain where all your inner reflections of reality are produced. You were taught that you are a human being living in a world that is separate from you and that you understand it through the activity that takes place in your brain.

This is one of the most foundational stories we've been told about who we are. I call it the story of the thinking-thing, and it is a model that we will be challenging deeply throughout this book. The story of the thinking-thing is a story we've lived inside of for a long time. It's been the source of magnificent human achievements, and it is currently the source of many of the global problems that we find ourselves unable to address.

The mind-bending insight I want to share is that we were not thinking-things that developed an understanding of ourselves and the world. We became thinking-things as we learned to think about ourselves as thinking-things, and then we created a world for thinking-things to live in. This means that if we change the way we think about ourselves we will become a different kind of being, and we can create a different kind of world.

So if reality is not a preexisting space to live in and understand, what is it? I would say that the best way to think about reality is to think about it as a range of possibility. That means that what is real is defined by what is possible. When we see ourselves as thinking-things, we place ourselves inside a range of possibility defined by what we believe is possible for the thinking-things that we think we are. That range defines our reality, and whatever might lie beyond it simply doesn't exist for us. In order to increase the amount of possibility available to us, we must move beyond our thinking-thing understanding of ourselves into an understanding that opens up a greater range of possibility. Ultimately the purpose of this book is to increase what is possible.

As I've already said, this book is a manual for engaging in the art of wormhole inquiry. This form of inquiry challenges our fundamental pictures and stories about reality. To engage in it all we have to do is simply contemplate an alternative understanding of reality and then ask ourselves if it might be true. Once we get to the point where we realize that indeed this new story about reality might be true, we can start asking ourselves how likely it is to be true. Eventually we compare it to our current understanding of reality and ask if the new possibility is as likely, or maybe even more likely, to be accurate.

If the alternative model is powerful enough and we pursue the inquiry long enough, we will find that it starts to look increasingly plausible. The true magic happens when you realize that the new model is just as likely to be true as the previous one. Suddenly you have two opposing models of reality that are equally plausible, and you are living in the magical space between them. You have your conventional understanding on one hand and an alternative under-standing on the other, and the facts of your experience are equally well explained by either.

Something mysterious happens at this profound point of equilibrium because suddenly you don't know which is true. You always believed in the conventional model of reality because it seemed so much more obviously true than any other possibility you could imagine. But now you have another model that fits the facts of your experience just as well. Suddenly you feel like you have a choice where there shouldn't be options. You have a choice between two different realities, but you've been taught that there is only one reality. Yet when you look, you realize that the new alternative is just as likely to be true as the original one.

This moment brings with it a deep sense of existential insecurity. It is the ultimate experience of the rug being pulled out from under your feet. We could say that it's the experience of having the reality pulled out from under your world. Most people don't have the strength and courage to stay this wide open and disoriented for long. We quickly become overwhelmed by the need for security and more often than not collapse into one or the other option and assert that it is the real reality.

If our temperament is more conservative, we dig our heels into the world we've known, and we risk falling into fundamentalism. If we do, we will reject the new possibility as fraudulent and dangerous and champion the stability and wisdom of the way things have been.

If our temperament is more progressive, we'll plant our stake in the new possibility and denigrate the previous way as outdated, ineffective, and dangerous. We risk becoming a zealot championing the power and brilliance of a new vision.

I don't believe that either of these positions is the gateway to a new paradigm because they both firmly rest in the assumption that one or the other is right and the other wrong. They still maintain the assumption of there being only one truth, which means they are both firmly rooted in the current paradigm. They both fit comfortably inside what we can know to be true.

The real opportunity of this disorienting experience occurs when we learn to rest in the radical uncertainty of that unknown place between both alternatives. We simply sit in the middle between two equally plausible models of reality until we start to become comfortable there. In this place you simply don't know what's true, and you stop trying to find out.

I would go so far as to say that not knowing what is true is not just the gateway to a different paradigm; it is the only experience of a different paradigm that we can currently have. We will never experience a new paradigm as something we can know. We will only be able to experience it as foreign and incomprehensible because to our current sensibilities that is what it is.

In any wormhole inquiry both of the two models of reality we start with—the conventional one and the alternative—are conceivable. So neither of them is likely to be the actual final form of a truly new paradigm. What is always more interesting than either of these two alternatives is the mysterious space between them. Between these two visions of reality lies a wormhole of impercept-ibility. When it emerges in our experience, it always appears as the unknowable, and it provides us the opportunity to rest in it and acclimate to the feeling of uncertainty it brings. To be an effective articulator of new paradigms or an artist of possibility, we must get used to the experience of living beyond understanding by resting in the insecurity of not knowing long enough to discover how to navigate from there.

If we can do this, we will find that something miraculous begins to happen. We won't just start understanding something new; we will start to experience a different way of knowing altogether. In the current paradigm we have always relied on our mental pictures and stories to tell us what is real and to guide our actions and choices in the world.

As we become increasingly comfortable in the unknown, we will begin to open into a different way of operating altogether. Profound powers of intuition will become available to us, and we will start to perceive things that we cannot see, hear, taste, touch, smell, or understand.

These new perceptions are not feelings in any common sense. They are much more subtle. They are a kind of knowing that has no basis and no foundation. They are not deductions or conclusions drawn from experience. They are direct sensibilities of a truth that appears whole and always just beyond our grasp.

I believe that a different paradigm for being human will emerge as more and more of us discover that we can perceive the imperceptible, know the unknowable, and see the invisible. As we learn to trust these mysterious perceptions as much as we trust our concrete conventional perception, our experience of reality will shift, and we will find ourselves responding to life in uncanny ways. Who we will become will arise out of the unknown space between worlds, and the things that we do and say from there will create a very different reality.

We've already said that we live inside a paradigm based on an assumption of separation and division. We've been trained to believe that we live *in* a reality that is separate from us. The reality that we live in is a universe of empty space populated by things that exist independent from one another. And because this is what we believe about the universe, it becomes how we experience the universe.

Before we go further, let's look again, even more closely, at the mechanisms through which paradigms operate. When we say we live in a paradigm, what we are saying is that we live inside a set of beliefs and assumptions, often unconscious, that tell us how to think about everything. These beliefs and assumptions shape our perception of reality so that we end up seeing things exactly the way we believed they were to begin with. What makes shifting paradigms so difficult is that the ideas of the paradigm shape our perception so that it continually matches and reinforces the same ideas that are doing the shaping in the first place.

A paradigm is a story about the way things are that shapes our perception so that it always matches the original story. No matter what we experience, a story will wrap around it and explain it in such a way that it fits in harmoniously with the preconceptions that were there to begin with. And as long as the world keeps showing up the way we think it should, we don't feel compelled to question anything.

Emotionally it is important to the human psyche that our experience of reality remains continuous. We have a deep allergic reaction to discontinuity. We want the present to be aligned with the past. We want to think that reality is ordered and predictable so we feel assured that the past will allow us to accurately guess what will happen in the future. If reality starts to feel discontinuous—if the future no longer feels like an inevitable outcome of the past—then there is no way for us to predict or control what will happen next.

This emotional need for continuity helps explain why paradigm-busting insights and ideas have historically been met with fervent opposition. In *The Structure of Scientific Revolutions*, Thomas Kuhn points out that the image of science as a progressive accumulation of increasingly accurate ideas about a single underlying reality is a myth.

The true history of science is a succession of paradigms. A shift in paradigm is not just a new set of ideas about the same world. A shift in paradigm is a shift into a new world altogether. Each new paradigm in the history of science is dominant for a time, until eventually its foundational assumptions are challenged and replaced by a new set of ideas. The reality described by this new set of ideas is profoundly different than the one it replaced. The true history of science, according to Kuhn, is more accurately described as a series of discontinuous leaps from one world to another. Only in retrospect do the authors of science texts rewrite history to construct a view that makes it look like the new paradigm was the inevitable outcome of progress that took us to a better under-standing of the same world that we were always in.

According to Kuhn, the development of science is punctuated by revolutionary leaps in understanding that leave unbridgeable gaps in the historical record. This is emotionally challenging because it implies that the reality of tomorrow may have little or nothing to do with the reality of today. It introduces an existential source of insecurity that is all but impossible for most of us to bear for longer than a few moments. Of course it is also what makes dramatic and sweeping change possible. Those of us who believe that our world needs a shift in paradigm are hoping for this kind of discontinuousness because we recognize that nothing less will be enough. If we see the limitations of the current paradigm and want to play a part in manifesting a new one, we must find the inner strength and emotional fortitude to face the insecurity of not knowing what tomorrow will bring. How terrifying and how exhilarating at the same time.

A paradigm shift is a discontinuous leap in logic and perception. The world before the shift is different from the world after. How is that possible? How can the world shift in an instant? You may find the idea challenging because it contradicts our cultural preference for a world that progresses slowly, orderly, incrementally, and, most importantly of all, predictably.

A new paradigm is coming; in fact it's been felt in the hearts and minds of forward-looking individuals for hundreds of years. Many of us today are committed to a new possibility and are busy exploring the ideas associated with it. Of course knowing about a new paradigm doesn't necessarily help us inhabit it, because our ideas, as new and exciting as they may be, are always expressed in language, and the language we use is always intimately tied into the story of the current paradigm. Inevitably, as soon as we start to explain the radical and revolutionary concept, the words and language we use to describe it have already started to encode it with the assumptions of the current paradigm.

Those of us who are committed to inhabiting the space of a new paradigm must find a way to embrace the existential insecurity of opening ourselves and moving beyond anything we can know. Which means going where our pictures and stories can't take us. As I have already discussed, there is a miraculous inner space that we can access when we open to the possibility of a future that is not limited by the past. In this space of uncertainty we honestly don't know what is possible, and so effectively anything is.

The inner landscape that we must enter into is a non-conceptual space of pure experience. In this space of experience without story we come into direct contact with raw uninterpreted reality. Here we find ourselves in direct contact with the sensual "stuff" out of which reality is made. It is like walking into a well-stocked art room and realizing you can create anything from the materials you find.

Once we have entered this space of unlimited possibility, we will be tempted to start creating right away, but if we do our creations will inevitably be circumscribed by the existing paradigm. We will at best be able to create better versions of what already exists. We cannot create a new paradigm because we are part of the story of the existing paradigm.

The self that we know ourselves to be is a subplot of the existing story of reality. We are a subroutine of the programming that runs the entire paradigm. We cannot, from the vantage point of the self that we know ourselves to be, usher in a new paradigm, because we ourselves are already an inseparable part of the current paradigm.

We cannot write the story of a new paradigm because we are part of the current paradigm, but the new paradigm can write its own story through us if we let it. Once we enter into the non-conceptual space of raw possibility, it is not our job to create. It is our sacred work to allow creation to happen through us. The expression may come through in words, images, or any other creative act, but the most important thing is that we let ourselves be moved by something beyond who we think we are. We are effectively allowing ourselves to be guided by the energy of a paradigm that is trying to find its way into this world. All we have to do is let it move us—let it speak with our voices, dance with our bodies, love with our hearts, and think with our minds.

If we can do this, if we can allow something that truly abides outside of the current paradigm to live through us, then we can become the medium for the articulation of a new paradigm. We are not the authors of a new paradigm. We are the space for its emergence, the blank page upon which the new story is yet to be written.

The story of a new paradigm is an autobiographical one because it must write itself into existence. No story that we can write will be it, and yet this self-authoring process requires our participation. It won't happen without us because our energy needs to be available for it. So as long as we are busy operating within the current paradigm of separation we are not available to be reconfigured into a paradigm of unity. It is up to us to disengage with the current paradigm and liberate our energy to be utilized by a process that will change who we are.

WORMHOLE INQUIRY

How do you enter non-conceptual space? How do you pass beyond the limits of your mind's knowing and understanding into a perception that is unknown and ultimately unknowable? How do you become the space of possibility out of which something truly novel can be born?

It is easier than you might assume—if you don't think about it!

Shifting into non-conceptual space is easy; resting there for any length of time is very difficult and usually takes years of practice. Luckily, in order to become an artist of possibility you don't need to be adept at resting in non-conceptual space. You only need to have access to it.

In this wormhole inquiry you will shift back and forth between two different possible realities. One is the normal conceptual reality that you know; the other is the non-conceptual reality that you will never know.

Try this. Look out at your surroundings, and without thinking about it just shift your awareness into the empty space of not knowing.

I am looking out at my living room. I see chairs, a table, a bookshelf with books on it, a staircase, etc. Just for a second I allow myself to forget what all the things are, and I just hover in the mystery of being. It doesn't feel like anything special. Just a sense of being without knowing.

The trick to this is not thinking about it. If you are trying to figure out how to do it, it won't work. If you are trying to figure out a technique that will do it, it won't work.

You just do it without knowing how to do it. Just instantaneously shift your attention from knowing to not knowing. From a world full of identified objects to seeing without knowing what you are seeing.

Keep trying it until you get the hang of it. Allow yourself to slip back and forth from the conceptual world that is familiar to the non-conceptual world that feels oddly like home.

As this shift becomes more comfortable to you, see if you can rest there for a second or two. Gradually, if you keep practicing, you will be able to abide in the non-conceptual awareness of pure experience for longer and longer periods of time.

This is the essence of meditation.

CHAPTER FOUR
THE MYTH OF
THE INDIVIDUAL ACHIEVER

We are exploring what it means and what it takes to shift paradigms. And ultimately we shall see that it is our sense of self that needs to change. We are not individuals stuck in a paradigm trying to get out; we ourselves are the paradigm that we long to shift out of.

At one level, as I've already said, we live inside of personal and cultural paradigms that shape our perceptions and behaviors, but at a deeper level we will find that being human is a story that is itself a paradigm that the consciousness of the universe is trapped inside of. We are on a quest to discover how to release the universe's awareness from the shape of being human, but first we need to explore in detail the paradigm of being human that is shaping us.

The paradigm that humanity and therefore the universe itself is currently embedded in—at least on this planet—could be called the *individual achiever paradigm*. In it we feel like separate individuals that generate achievements by setting goals, creating plans, and realizing them through willful acts. We see ourselves as entities that roam the earth manifesting our dreams and desires through our own effort.

This seems obvious. We look at ourselves, and what we see is an individual achieving things in the world. So naturally we assume that because that is the way it looks, that must be the way it is.

What we often don't realize is that just because we feel like an individual achiever doesn't mean that we are one.

What makes paradigm shifting so tricky is that we are trained to more or less assume that things are the way they appear to be. We have been trained to think that we see a reality that exists independently of us when in fact the reality that we see is shaped by the assumptions, beliefs, and mental processes of perception that we see with. These influences act like a lens that shapes our experience of reality. This lens is what a paradigm is.

In the current paradigm, we have been taught that our brains are information-processing machines that take in information about the world through our five senses. Once the information has been collected, it is filtered and arranged into a comprehensible picture of reality—a reality that we assume was already there before we started collecting data about it. We believe that the picture of reality that our minds create is an accurate representation of what is real.

Ontology is the branch of philosophy that is concerned with how to determine when something gets to count as real. The most accepted means of determining truth today is through the accumulation of observable and preferably measurable evidence.

Unfortunately—and here is the trick—any proof that we find is being gathered through the very same filter of mind that we are seeing through in the first place. It is like looking through blue-colored glasses and then believing that because everything looks blue, everything must be blue. Unless you can take the glasses off, you will never be able to know what the world really looks like.

There are lots of things you can know about the world while wearing blue glasses. You can know how tall buildings are, how fast you're moving, how many pickles there are in a bushel, but you can't know anything about color that isn't shaped by the glasses you're wearing.

The theory of mind that we have been trained in is called the representational model of mind. We have been taught that reality preexists our experience of it and that our senses act like a mirror that reflects it back to us so we can see it. Because this is what we have been taught, we assume that things are the way they appear to be—at least more or less. So when we see ourselves as individuals who set goals, create plans, and achieve things, we assume that must be who we are.

What if we only experience reality that way because our perception is being shaped by the preconception that we are that way? What if we are wearing individual achiever–colored glasses and so we see ourselves and everyone else as individual achievers? We look around, and it looks obvious that we are individual achievers because that is all we see. Just like looking around and seeing the world is blue and assuming that it must be that way.

The philosopher Alfred North Whitehead said, "It requires a very unusual mind to undertake the analysis of the obvious." I believe what he meant was that much of what is obvious to us only appears obvious because of the preconscious filtering mechanisms of our minds. Examining this filtering system is like using the mind to see itself—and this takes an extraordinary effort.

So what might an alternative to the individual achiever be?

At one time I worked as a school teacher, and from time to time I would show nature documentaries to my classes, and of all the ones I ever watched my favorite was about North American beaver ponds, and it explored the ecosystem that emerges around these ponds.

Beavers are famed as the creatures that chop down trees and use the logs to build dams in streams and rivers. Once the flow of the water has been stopped, a pond forms. These beaver ponds become the home of a diverse number of species of plants and animals, and they all depend on the dam. The beavers maintain a home for all of these species by continuously repairing the dam anytime the water overruns it.

As young children, we might imagine that beavers love to chop wood and create ponds. And if we look we can find evidence that supports this reality. Everywhere they exist, beavers chop wood and build dams that create ponds. It certainly looks like they love doing it.

In the documentary they give a more scientific explanation. It seems that beavers find the sound of running water deeply agitating, and whenever they hear it they start building dams to stop the sound. This has been studied by playing recordings of running water and finding that the beavers start working on the dam as soon as they hear the recording even though there is no actual water running. So it seems they are not building a dam to stop water and maintain a pond. They just want some peace and quiet.

Notice that both explanations are supported by evidence. The problem with evidence-based assessments of truth is that the same facts can be interpreted in different ways to lead to different conclusions about what is real. And all of the interpretations and the conclusions they lead to will look equally real.

Let's present a third interpretation of the facts of the beaver pond—one that is fundamentally different from the two above and yet equally well supported by the facts of the matter. Before we introduce this third interpretation, please notice that both the child's and the scientist's interpretations above happen inside the individual achiever paradigm. That means that in both explanations we assume that the beaver pond is being formed by the beavers in an effort to fulfill their own needs.

What if we don't assume that the beaver is the agent of the action? When we look at the ecosystem that forms around the beaver pond, what we see are frogs and deer and flowers and trees that all start to thrive because the water has been stopped.

The child might think that beavers love the animals and plants so much that they want to create a home for them. The scientist thinks that the beavers have an intolerance for the sound of rushing water and don't care at all about the pond that forms or the ecosystem it supports.

In either case the focus is on the beavers. What if we look at things from the ecosystem's point of view? What if the ecosystem is the real agent? What if the beavers are intolerant of the sound of running water because the ecosystem needs them to be? What if we imagine that the ecosystem is calling itself into existence by making the beavers irritated at the sound of rushing water?

From the beavers' point of view it feels like they can't stand the sound of rushing water, but looking from the ecosystem's vantage point the beaver needs to feel that way so the pond can form and the ecosystem can thrive. What if the ecosystem was driving the whole process and not the beavers? Picture the ecosystem as if it were like the conductor of an orchestra busily orchestrating itself into existence.

It is easier for us to embrace the scientific explanation and assume that the beaver is an individual achiever that incidentally plays a part in a bigger picture. It is harder to imagine that something as intangible as an ecosystem is orchestrating the whole event. But if we do, something interesting happens. We start to feel the actions of the beaver being guided by the intelligence that resides in the entire ecosystem. The beaver is not the acting agent. The ecosystem is acting through the beaver.

The reason it is harder for us to believe in the second explanation is because it is not aligned with our individual achiever sensibilities. But I encourage you to imagine that the ecosystem is the intelligence that is operating through the beavers. Then look at your own actions and activities and think about what higher form of intelligence might be acting through you. Maybe you, like the beaver, are not the active agent. Then what is it that is guiding your actions?

WORMHOLE INQUIRY

Take a moment to think of something you did today. Maybe you read a newspaper or ate a meal. Now analyze that activity through your normal individual achiever lens. That means thinking about why you did what you did. What was the objective of the activity? What did you want to achieve?

You wanted to find out what was happening in the news, so you read a newspaper.

You were hungry and wanted to feel satisfied, so you ate.

Now see if there is some way that you can see this same activity from the point of view of some larger acting agent.

Maybe the events of the world want to be known, and so they compel you to read about them. Maybe the food on your plate wants to be digested so that it will become energy that can move more easily through the universe.

Maybe there is a future possibility that wants to come into existence, and you are destined to play a key role in it, so the future itself is compelling you to eat and be healthy.

Of course all of the interpretations of some agent of action bigger than us will sound implausible—but is that because they are? Or do they sound that way because we have become so used to assuming that we are an acting agent that we can't imagine it any other way?

Is it really so impossible that there might be a source of intelligence larger than human intelligence in this universe that is acting through us? What is it that makes that so impossible?

Are there some sets of facts that can't be made to fit that interpretation and therefore make it impossible to be true? What are those facts?

Why is it impossible that the activities of the world want to be known? Or the food on your plate wants to be turned into energy?

Isn't the reason that these things feel impossible because we experience the inside of our own minds and not the minds of worldly activities or meals on plates?

If we were to experience a carrot's desire to have the energy trapped in its physical form released, we might look at it differently. We might see it purposefully sitting there on the plate looking delicious trying to get us to eat it.

Now remember, this is a wormhole inquiry, so you don't need to prove that carrots want to be eaten. You only have to examine hard enough to see that it is possible that there are other forms of intelligence in the universe that are acting besides human beings. Then just rest in the betweenness of recognizing that you don't really know which is true.

PART TWO
THE EVOLUTION OF REALITY

In this section of the book we will embark upon a series of philosophical investigations and wormhole inquiries designed to free us from the assumptions of the current paradigm and free our awareness to embrace a radical alternative.

CHAPTER FIVE
FROM INDIVIDUAL ACHIEVEMENT
TO UNIVERSAL EMERGENCE

We are all born into a preexisting paradigm, and that paradigm consists of all of the unconscious assumptions we hold that tell us what is real and how reality works. In the last chapter we determined that one of the most foundational assumptions we hold is that we operate in the world through the power of individual achievement.

We see ourselves as beings that effect change by making independent decisions and then acting on them. We operate by using our minds to imagine new possibilities; then we set goals, create plans, and take action to achieve our goals.

Of course we all know the world pushes back. Our goals are not always achieved in spite of our best effort. Things happen that thwart our plans, and sometimes we discover that other people are busy enacting plans of their own that counter ours. And yet, we go on day after day, imagining new possibilities and strategizing how to bring them to life.

This happens in small ways like when we imagine milk in our refrigerator and decide to walk to the store on the corner to get some. It also happens in big ways like when we decide to become a doctor and contemplate which colleges and universities we should attend to make that dream come true.

Paradigms are multi-layered. They are not simply composed of a jumble of assumptions and assertions. The beliefs and attitudes that make up a paradigm are layered one upon the other. More superficial elements are closer to the surface and easier to uncover. The deeper you go into the belief system, the more ubiquitous are the assumptions you find. Uncovering the deeper layers of assumption means we can catalyze much bigger shifts.

Shifting your paradigm can dramatically expand the range of possibility available to you. The deeper the shift in the paradigm, the greater the expansion of possibility. I call paradigm shifters artists of possibility because they are literally creating more possibility in the world. To illustrate, let's imagine someone who is planning to attend Harvard Medical School in Massachusetts because their mother and father are both doctors who graduated from Harvard. This aspiring medical student has assumed that they would go to Harvard to study medicine for as long as they can remember.

We could see this as an example of someone living in a paradigm. Now let's imagine that person starts to question going to Harvard. Suddenly a new range of possibility opens to them. They could go to Stanford in California or Rice University in Texas. They could even go to a university in a country outside the United States.

If they questioned a little more deeply, they might wonder if they should be a doctor in the first place. Suddenly they could be an artist or a carpenter or a circus performer. Maybe they would travel to India to seek enlightenment. The range of possibility would open up much wider because they had questioned more deeply.

Our Western culture currently has an influence, for better and worse, that spreads across the entire globe. Many of us see that we have reached the limits of what I'm now calling the independent achiever paradigm. It seems that this paradigm is no longer capable of effectively responding to the complexity of the world as it is. The massive impact that human beings who are living through this paradigm are having on the ecology of this planet, and the precarious state of the social and economic systems that support human life, make it clear that something big needs to change. We simply cannot find a way to effectively navigate into the future from inside our current individual achiever operating system.

My assertion is that the foundational assumption that we are "individuals achieving goals" has to be questioned. As soon as we open up this line of questioning, we see how embedded we are in the current paradigm. After all, isn't the desire to shift into a new paradigm just another goal that I'm trying to achieve?

How is it possible to question the existing paradigm when we are so embedded in it? What kinds of questions can an individual achiever ask that will lead to the realization that they are not an individual achiever asking questions?

We need to look far beneath the assumption of being an individual achiever because there is a much deeper assumption that the idea of being an individual achiever rests on. The assumption of being an individual achiever rests on the deeper assumption that I am thinking my own thoughts. My belief in the independence of my cognitive faculties is one of the pillars upon which the whole house of cards of individual existence rests.

We commonly speak of my mind, my thoughts, my feelings, my ideas, etc. But what makes us believe they belong to us? One of the main reasons we think this is because we experience them and no one else does. So we assume they happen inside of us, and because they happen inside us we assume they belong to us.

It is interesting to consider that people didn't always experience an inner world of personal thoughts and feelings. It appears to be obvious to us, but it hasn't necessarily been obvious to everyone, everywhere, all the time. At different periods of human history and in some cultures today, people experience those "inner" voices as coming from outside of themselves, originating in spirits or deities, or from the animals and plants of the earth.

We tend to think of this as a primitive and less-developed point of view, but maybe it's just different. The idea that our thoughts come from outside of us seems superstitious to our modern Western sensibilities, but that's because there was a concerted effort to make it seem that way as Western culture moved from the Middle Ages into the Enlightenment.

If we start to ask the right questions, we can make our common perception of a private inner world start to look arbitrary and almost random. Let's make an analogy with me typing this book. Right now my fingers are typing out these words, but no one thinks that my fingers are writing this essay. We aren't about to list the author as Jeff's fingers. We've all been trained to think that I, Jeff, am writing these words and that my fingers are a part of me—one of my possessions.

Similarly, if we were talking together right now, it would be obvious to both of us that the conversation was more than my mouth talking to your ears. It is the whole of me talking to the whole of you. The mouth and the ears are just parts of us that are involved in the process of talking, but they are not "doing" anything; they are just functioning.

It is obvious as soon as we look that the lines of division that appear to separate our fingers, mouths, and ears from the rest of us are not real in the sense that those parts of us do not have an existence independent from us. And yet we do believe in the line that separates the whole of me from the rest of the world. On what grounds do we hold that the division that defines me is real and creates a truly independent entity, while the lines that separate all of the parts of me are not real?

Why am I separate from the ground under my feet? Or the air that I breathe? Or the food that I eat?

We can't exist without those things. How long would we survive floating out in space?

Physically we are inextricably one with this planet. Why would we assume that we are mentally separate?

Now let's turn our attention to the nature and origins of our thinking. When I walk outside and think about what a beautiful sunny day it is, am I having a thought independent from the beautiful sunny day? Would that thought arise in me on a cloudy day? Is that thought arising in me separate from the day itself, or is the thought an aspect of the day?

Your thoughts, feelings, and emotions never arise in isolation— they always arise in relationship to something. The circumstances that give rise to thoughts might be physical like walking outside on a beautiful day, or they might be the mental circumstances created by memories, feelings, or other thoughts. No matter where they come from, thoughts don't just appear magically out of thin air. They emerge out of the circumstances we find ourselves in.

The new paradigm will include a deep recognition of the fact that everything that exists comes into existence as part of a larger circumstance. To initiate a shift into this paradigm of interdependence, we must question our assumptions of separation so deeply that we shift our perception of reality altogether. Our nervous systems need to be rewired so that we experience ourselves as beings emerging out of circumstances rather than isolated entities acting upon a world that is separate from us. We must learn to see everything that we create and achieve as an extension of the circumstances that surround us rather than personal achievements of our own.

This shift in perception requires that we continue to dissolve all of the imagined boundaries that limit us until we discover that ultimately there is no boundary that separates anything from anything else. As we let go of more and more of the assumptions that isolate us, we will feel oneness with all that is.

We will not just know that all is one; we will see it, and we will feel it. In a way that we cannot yet imagine, we will experience the rippling effects of our being through the universe and at the same time experience the universe itself rippling through us. We will have become universal beings to the degree that we live within a recognition of continuity with all of existence. We will no longer experience ourselves making independent decisions in isolation from each other, the world, or the universe. We will realize that we are being moved in accordance with universal prompts. We will become inseparably whole.

WORMHOLE INQUIRY

Here is a thought experiment to give you a more visceral sense that you are not separate from the world. All you have to do is imagine leaving this planet and going into space.

The first thing to consider is that you can't do it at all unless you have a pressurized suit. Otherwise the oxygen in your blood will boil and generate air bubbles. That's because normally you exist inside the pressure of the Earth's atmosphere. You were born under pressure, and you can't survive without it because it holds you together. Of course you also need oxygen to breathe, so that has to be pumped into your suit. If you want to spend more than a few hours in space, you'll need water too, and it will be hard to take much without a spaceship. To stay even longer you'll need food, and for any extensive stay you'll need to grow food, which means bringing light and soil with you as well.

Do you see what you end up doing? You have to recreate the Earth and Sun. You have to bring the whole planet out into space with you. Why? Because you can't exist separate from the planet, because you aren't separate from the planet. You weren't just born on the planet; you were born part of it.

You've been taught to think of yourself as a thing, but in fact in many ways you are much more like a bubble. Your body is like a bubble—a bubble of gas and liquid held in place by the air around you.

Think about an air bubble in a glass of water. You can see it in the water, but you can't take it out. Air bubbles don't exist separate from water. Air bubbles out of water are just air.

Think about the fact that, like an air bubble, you don't exist outside of the world. They say a person would survive no more than fifteen seconds in the vacuum of space. That's how long you can exist independently of this planet.

Yet in our everyday life as we walk around on the surface of the Earth we feel separate from it. We feel like an isolated self-contained thing, but we're not. We are not a thing that walks around on a planet. We are a highly organized system of organs, tissues, and fluids held together by the air around us and energized by sunlight trapped in the plants we eat.

Can you start to see your inseparable oneness with the earth?

CHAPTER SIX
A STORYBOOK UNIVERSE

Most, if not all, of the people reading this book will be reading it from inside the paradigm of the modern Western world. That paradigm has often been seen as rooted in scientific materialism and is sometimes called the Cartesian-Newtonian paradigm, named after two of its most prominent originators, René Descartes and Sir Isaac Newton.

From inside this paradigm the universe is recognized to be an infinite expanse of empty three-dimensional space filled with things. And we see ourselves as complex biological organisms with nervous systems sophisticated enough to make us conscious. In other words, we see ourselves as thinking things.

Inside the current paradigm we are trained to relate to our experience as if it were an accurate representation of reality. We believe our senses are giving us information that reflects the truth of the way things are when in fact everything we experience has been previously shaped by our things-in-space assumptions.

Paradigms don't present themselves as ideas about reality. They present themselves as reality itself. Finding your way out of a paradigm feels like finding your way out of reality. It feels impossible because we believe that reality as we currently experience it is all there is.

As far as we can see, there is the real and the unreal. The real exists, and the unreal does not. So our deep assumption will be that there is nothing to find outside of the reality of the current paradigm.

Let's go through this slowly. What we see as reality is not necessarily real. What we see as reality is a perception created in large part by the assumptions we hold about reality. These assumptions come to us from the current paradigm and then end up feeling like reality.

We experience sensations that get shaped into perceptions of the world. If I look outside the window, all I actually see are shapes and colors, but if you ask me what I'm looking at, I will say a brick building with a tree in front of it.

None of us really sees buildings or trees. We see shapes and colors that our minds put together into experiences of buildings and trees, but what we assume is that we see buildings and trees. A paradigm is the set of instructions that tells our minds how to shape all of our perceived sensations into an experience of reality.

It gets even trickier because the paradigm not only dictates how the mind shapes our experience of reality, it also insists that the mind only recognize things shaped that way as real. In effect a paradigm tells you how to look at things and then tells you that only things that look that way are real.

A paradigm is a sort of circular argument that catches us in a loop by asserting that its premise is evidence of its validity. Here's an example of a circular argument that will illustrate how it works.

1. That politician is a great communicator.

2. How do you know?

3. Because she communicates so well.

That argument doesn't prove anything. All that's been said is that something is true because it's true. Similarly a paradigm shapes your experience into a particular form and then tells you that that form is real because you experience it that way.

Of course a paradigm is not an entity giving instructions. So what is it?

A paradigm lives in the stories we tell ourselves about what is real.

We may indeed live in a universe of material things, but just as much we live in a universe made up of stories, that are inside other stories, that are inside other stories, etc. — a storybook universe.

The current paradigm is a story about an infinite expanse of three-dimensional space filled with things. Inside that story there is a story about a planet called Earth and another story about a particular species on that planet called humans that think. Then there is a story about a particular individual member of that species called Jeff, who sometimes writes books like this one.

Everything that exists is a story about something that exists. You might not believe this and want to say that there are things that exist that are not just stories about things that exist. My blue jeans are not just a story about a garment of clothes. They are actual clothes made of undeniably real atoms and molecules.

First of all I would want to say that my blue jeans, like the building and tree earlier on, are just colors, shapes, and textures that I amalgamate into the idea of blue jeans. As far as the atoms and molecules are concerned, they are part of the story of the scientific materialist paradigm that says there are things called atoms and molecules that everything else is made of.

The storybook universe is made up of stories inside of stories inside of stories all the way through. Nothing but stories, and anytime you look to find something beyond all the stories all you will find are stories about what lies beyond all the other stories.

This may start to feel infuriating because it is another example of a circular argument. I tell you that everything is a story, and then no matter what you say in response I point out how that is also a story. And this is exactly how paradigms work. They start with an initial premise that gets projected outward until it is all you see. Then the fact that all you see is the original premise is used as proof that the original premise must be true.

You might concede that I have made my point about the circular nature of paradigms, but the storybook version of reality just seems silly because to adopt it you have to leave so many things unexplained. One of the biggest complaints being that if reality is just a set of stories, and I am just a story, then who is telling all the stories? I can't tell you where the stories are coming from, or who is telling them, or who is hearing them—except of course to tell you more stories.

But the current scientific paradigm also leaves many things unexplained. It is based on a belief that space is infinite in three dimensions, which can't be explained. It insists that there are indivisible units of matter that the universe is built from without explaining where those units come from. It tells a story about a Big Bang without explaining what was there before that or how that initial explosion was ignited. The current paradigm can't explain where life came from or what consciousness is either, but when we live inside it we are very willing to forgive these omissions while insisting that any alternative explanation must be fully explained through and through.

A paradigm can explain everything inside itself, but it can never explain the assumptions it is built on. Once a paradigm becomes widely accepted, those living inside it simply forget about the unexplained premises, or leave a few people at the edges to keep working to figuring them out.

The point is that the premise of a storybook universe is just as plausible as the premise of a things-in-space universe.

We live in a universe that is stories all the way through. Stories that are not just reports on real things, but are actually shaping what we experience as real. Each story shapes things in a particular way until the experience of this moment is the way it is because of the overlapping stories that influence it.

We live in a universe made of stories, and one of those stories is a story about living in a universe made of things in space. It is interesting to note that even our scientists know this story isn't the whole story. More importantly, when we see that we live in a reality made of stories, we find that moving out of our current reality into a new one is just a matter of shifting into a new story.

WORMHOLE INQUIRY

In this wormhole inquiry I want you to identify something around you. Just pick something—a book, a chair, a tree, the sun, a person—anything. Once you have something in mind, think about what it is. If it is a book, think about what a book is. It has pages; it contains words; it is published. Think about everything you know about the book or whatever item you picked.

Contemplate the fact that the thing you picked, whatever it is, is really a story. It is a story about the thing. It is the story that tells you what the object is made of, what it is used for, how it is used, what it does, how it affects things, etc. Whatever you chose it will turn out to be a story.

Then ask yourself the question, if you had a book in your hand but you knew absolutely nothing about what a book was, would it still be a book? If you didn't know what it was and you didn't know anything about language or reading, would you still have a book in your hand?

Keep looking around and choosing different objects one at a time. Think about everything you know about the things you choose. You will see that the stories you have about each of the common things around you is extensive.

I am sitting at a table. I know it is made of wood. I have some idea of how wood is harvested and how it is turned into boards in a lumber yard. I have some experience building things with wood. I have used a hammer and a saw. All of these things and much, much more are embedded in my recognition of what a table is.

If you take the objects that you are thinking about and strip away all of the story you know about them, if you allow them to become utterly unfamiliar, what is left? You still have an object in your hand. You still have your experience of the thing—the hardness, the smoothness, the temperature, and the color, but what is it?

If you strip away all of the stories about an object, isn't the only thing you have left the pure non-conceptual experience of it?

CHAPTER SEVEN
THINKING THE THOUGHTS
OF THE UNIVERSE

As we have already established, in the current paradigm of being human we are trained to think of ourselves according to the story of being an individual achiever. That means we imagine that we are isolated individual beings who run around with brains processing information and making decisions.

In this paradigm we see ourselves as the initiators of the actions we take. We are choosers and actors making independent decisions. This belief gives us a strong sense of freewill, personal power, and self-determination. We feel like doers.

What we miss in this view is the fact that we are part of a larger process of life. We are not the beginning of everything that happens. We arrived in the middle of a process that has been in operation for longer than we can imagine.

Earlier I asserted that the assumption of being an individual achiever rested on the even more deeply held assumption that we are thinking our own thoughts. Now we are in a position to explore exactly what this means and why it is important.

When we think, we most commonly think of ourselves as being the originators of the thoughts. To us thinking thoughts means creating thoughts in our minds. But if you reflect on it, you will find that this is not really the way it happens. When you think, are you really creating thoughts? How do you do that?

If you really stop and look, you actually don't know where your thoughts are coming from. During the activity that we call thinking, we turn our attention inward and look at a process of "thinking" that is already going on. Thinking is already in process, but we have been taught that thinking means generating thoughts that don't yet exist and then choosing the best ones to act on.

So I ask you again, how do you think a thought? Do you really know where your thoughts are coming from? Do you really create them, or do they appear all by themselves?

As an analogy let's think about flavors. When we taste something, we don't think that the flavor is something we are doing. We aren't flavoring. We are tasting flavors that already exist in the thing we are tasting. In the same way, when we think we aren't really thinking; we are seeing thoughts that already exist in the things we are giving our attention to.

Here's an experiment to do. Think a thought right now and watch what happens. Do you think a thought, or do you look for one?

When I do this experiment, I find myself looking for a thought, not thinking it. What I seem to do is move my attention inward. I stop looking at the computer I'm typing on or the coffee shop around me and turn my gaze toward the inner world of thought and feeling. I seem to scan around my inner experience until a thought appears, and I never know exactly which one it will be until I see it.

When I looked just now, I saw this thought: "That tree outside is a magical shade of yellow."

The tree outside was the last thing I had seen before I decided to think a thought, and when I looked inside, I saw a thought about the tree.

You see, thoughts don't appear out of nowhere. They come attached to things. I could decide that the thought I just had was created in my head, but it is just as accurate to say it emerged out of the tree. Maybe thoughts are not created in our minds. Maybe they emerge out of things.

Maybe thinking is not something we do as much as it is something that happens. We appear to direct our attention toward the thought stream in our heads, but thoughts are not really things that we manufacture. They appear spontaneously in relationship to other aspects of our experience.

The whole world—inner and outer—is constantly leaking thoughts.

Here is another experiment. Look at something near you. Keep your attention on the details of whatever thing you are looking at and see what thoughts start to emerge.

I am looking at the building across the street, and I see thoughts emerging about bricks and the people living in the building and about how warm it is inside on this blustery day. I don't look at the brick building and have thoughts about penguins.

Ha! you might say, I got you. You just did have a thought about penguins.

Yes, I did have a thought about penguins while looking at that building, but the reason I did is because I was not just looking at the building. I was looking at it in the context of thinking about the point I am trying to illustrate.

So while I looked at the building I also looked for a random thought to use in the sentence above, and whenever I think of randomness I think of penguins.

Why?

I think of penguins in relationship to randomness because when I was young I used to play a game called "random thoughts." A friend and I would take turns saying a word, and then my friend would spontaneously come up with a word that had no relation at all to the one he had just heard.

My friend was great at that game, and I loved playing. Once in response to something I said he shouted out, "Penguins!" so fast that I was in awe of his creative mind. I never forgot that moment, and so I always associate randomness with penguins.

The point is that thoughts always grow out of preexisting experience. They emerge out of sights, sounds, feelings, or other thoughts. They are not produced independently in isolation, and we do not manufacture them in our heads out of thin air. In Buddhist philosophy this view is known as "dependent origination."

When I think, I am not creating thoughts; I am looking for them. Thoughts spontaneously appear in the mind constantly all by themselves. When we engage in the activity we know as thinking, we simply direct some of our attention toward an inner stream of thoughts that is always there.

We are trained to imagine that we think by manufacturing thoughts and using them to navigate life and make decisions.

But if you look, it is just as accurate to say that the thoughts in your head are emerging out of the objects in your experience. All of the objects in the universe—whether they be inner objects like emotions, memories, and thoughts or outer objects like trees and buildings—are all constantly leaking thoughts that we become aware of when we think.

Our minds don't think thoughts. They see thoughts that are emerging out of things.

In the current paradigm we have been trained to see most of the universe as dead and unconscious and ourselves as alive and intelligent.

Maybe it is the other way around. Maybe the world and everything in it is alive and intelligent. Maybe everything is constantly thinking thoughts that we then see with our minds. Maybe we don't think. Maybe the universe thinks and we are seeing the thoughts of a universal mind.

This way of interpreting the world is reminiscent of the worldview of indigenous cultures where the shaman, or holy person, would listen for the wisdom emerging out of the world around them. To these people everything was a living being that had wisdom to share.

This is also the way the German literary figure Johann Wolfgang von Goethe envisioned doing science. He had a competing view of science that is very different from the science we know today that was derived from people like Sir Isaac Newton. Where Newton wanted to understand everything by describing it in measurable and quantifiable terms, Goethe wanted to do science by observing things so deeply that they revealed their true nature to us. Goethe's way of doing science was much more like the science of the shaman.

Perhaps we need to go back to the wisdom of the shaman and the science of Goethe and see if we can shift the way we experience the world. Perhaps we need to retrain ourselves into seeing that intelligence belongs to the universe, not only to human beings.

Maybe if we didn't see ourselves as living and intelligent things in a mostly dead and unconscious universe we would find it easier to treat our planet like the living being that it is. This shift in paradigm is at least worth trying, and it might be essential for our future.

WORMHOLE INQUIRY

Take a moment to look at something, anything—a tree, a bookshelf, a cup of coffee. Just look at it without trying to think about anything and see what thoughts arise in you.

This will be difficult because you are so used to thinking that you are actively thinking your thoughts. This habit of being "the thinker" means that we are almost constantly manipulating thoughts. Trying to think specific thoughts.

If you sit and relax, that mental activity will give way, and you will start to just watch your mind generate thoughts about the object in front of you. Maybe it is a coffee cup that you received for your birthday. You might remember the person who gave it to you. Perhaps they were a coworker at your previous job. Then an image of your old office will emerge, and that will remind you of the work you used to do, which will remind you of the shift you made to your new job. Then you will wonder if your new job is really making you as happy as you thought it would. The thoughts will keep streaming through you for as long as you look at the cup.

Once you have performed this exercise for a while, stop and reflect on everything that arose in mind from looking at the object in front of you. Can you see all of that mental activity, not as you thinking about the cup, which is our habitual way of looking at it, but as the cup thinking through you? Sit for a while longer contemplating the fact that everything that arose in you while you looked at the coffee cup is exactly what the cup wanted to say to you.

Now move on to another object. Look at it and let it speak to you. What does the tree want to say? How about the bookshelf?

Can you see that everything is always communicating with you?

We are trained to see the things around us as inanimate and unintelligent, but isn't that just an assumption?

Isn't it just as congruent with the facts to assume that all of the things around us are communicative—that they are alive and intelligent?

CHAPTER EIGHT
WHAT IF NO ONE IS HAVING
THE EXPERIENCE YOU THINK
YOU'RE HAVING

In the second part of this book I see myself following in the footsteps of two of my true philosophical inspirations, Charles Sanders Peirce and William James. Hopefully by the end I will journey a step or two further along the trail that they originally blazed. Just after the American Civil War, Peirce and James became part of an amateur philosophical group called the Metaphysical Club. The expressed intention of this group was to expand on the idea of evolution described in Charles Darwin's *On the Origin of Species.* Darwin, according to the members of the Metaphysical Club, had not taken his ideas far enough. He described the mechanism through which species evolve one into the other, but why did he stop there when everything must have evolved, not just animal species on earth? In fact, they imagined, even the laws of time and space that we experience as the backdrop to everything else must themselves have come into being gradually through a process of evolution.

This book might rightly be considered to be part of the canon of what has come to be called evolutionary spirituality. Evolutionary spirituality is a spiritual philosophy rooted in the realization that we are part of an evolving universe and that our experience of consciousness is the consciousness of the universe itself in human form. Evolutionary spirituality is often associated with the pioneering work of the Jesuit priest and paleontologist Pierre Teilhard de Chardin. What is less well known is that on a long train ride from Paris to China (where he had been sent by the church in an attempt to get him to stop his pesky philosophizing) Teilhard brought along with him the collected works of Charles Sanders Peirce to read on the way.

It is my opinion that many more recent articulations of evolutionary spirituality miss the truly paradigm-shifting nature of the vision of conscious evolution that was articulated by people like Peirce, James, and Teilhard, because they can too easily be interpreted as a story told from the point of view of the separate sense of self. The "universe story," as it is sometimes referred to, is not a story about individual entities that call themselves human who realize that they are part of the story of the universe. The universe's story is a story about how an all-encompassing awareness that existed beyond time and space began to find expression of itself through a multitude of thought forms. And how one of those thought forms eventually attained a degree of self-awareness that allowed it to act as a platform for further consciousness. As the universal awareness passed through this form, it called itself human and mistakenly limited itself to being human. It is the story of how a universal awareness got lost in an identity that separated it from who and what it truly was. The paradigm-shifting journey that I am describing in this book is ultimately not the journey that human beings take to recognize that they are the universe. It is the journey the universe takes to discover that it is more than human.

The big difficulty in telling this story is the challenge with pronouns. Every time I refer to *I, we* or *you*, those little words tend to plant our feet right back in the current paradigm. *I, we* or *you* always defaults to the individual sense of self, the ego, that we think we are. So a sentence like,

You are the universe awakening to your own existence.

Is going to be interpreted as: I, the one who is a thinking-thing with a name, am realizing that I am in fact the universe awakening to myself. What if on the other hand we assume that the pronoun *you* in that sentence is not you, the one with the name, but you the universe itself? Try reading the same sentence above ten times in a row really trying to feel the "you" as the universe.

If you keep doing this, you will start to feel a shift in your sense of identity. You will start to feel that this sentence was not written for the person with the name. It was written for the universe. It is not a call for you, the one with the name, to awaken to your true identity. It is a call to the universe to awaken from the dream of being you, the one with the name. The book that you are holding in your hand has only one intended reader—the universe. And the universe is reading the book right now through your eyes. This book isn't really for you, although you are a necessary surrogate reader.

Now of course it is one thing to understand this as an intellectual idea. It is something else entirely to experience it, to realize that you are it. We can understand the idea of evolutionary spirituality without needing to leave the paradigm of separation. It is not so difficult to be a thinking-thing that gains a new idea about itself, but our world needs us to go beyond understanding.

We have been busy opening up new perceptual possibilities by questioning some of the unquestioned assumptions of the current paradigm. One of the deepest questions that we have asked is, Are my thoughts really mine? There turns out to be an even more foundational assumption underlying the current paradigm. That assumption is the belief that there is a reality that all of our thoughts that we assume are ours are about. The question we will be asking now is, Does anything real exist?

We've been taught that underneath all of our experiences there is a reality, a solid something that existed before we arrived and will exist long after we're gone. The reality that underlies our experience is like the precious metal that used to back up our currency. The fact that there is something standing behind it is what makes our experience worth something. We've also been trained to assume that there is only one reality. The assumption that only one thing can be real tends to make us absolutists. When we know something, we are quick to assume that we have the correct view of reality and everyone else must be wrong. The belief in one reality also makes us slow to transform because the underlying assumption is that reality is something that doesn't change.

As an example, people believed that the earth was flat for centuries. No one felt they needed to prove it because all you had to do was look out over the horizon and it was obvious. For a long, long time ships would veer away from the horizon in order to avoid going over the edge of the earth. Once we concluded that the earth was flat, there was no reason to question it since reality doesn't change.

The assumption that there is only one reality is a philosophical predisposition that has a firm grip on the Western psyche. We gain a great deal of comfort from the unquestioned assumption that underneath all of our ideas about reality there is in fact a reality that they are about. We sleep more soundly each night knowing that reality will still be there waiting for us when we open our eyes each morning. We want to question the assumed stability of reality, and once again we will be following the lead of Charles Sanders Peirce, who definitely had a mind unusual enough to question even something as obvious as this.

Peirce worked for the Coast Guard mapping the ocean floor. The mapping process involved dropping plumb lines to measure the depth of water in different spots and then generating a relief map from the data. He was an expert in measurement and logic. He was aware, as any scientist would be, that when you make the same measurement more than once you typically get different results. This is especially true if you are trying to make measurements that are very precise.

The obvious reason for the difference in our measurements is human error. We all learned this in our high school science classes. You are always asked to take multiple measurements and then use the average of them in your calculations. It is assumed that the average of multiple measurements will give a more reliable result because any single measurement in isolation might be off.

Peirce wondered about this, and his very unusual mind came up with a different, equally plausible explanation. Maybe our measurements are not in error. Maybe the things we are measuring are fluctuating, and every time we measure something we get a different measurement because the thing itself has changed.

Peirce spent his lifetime attempting to develop a philosophy that could describe a reality that was not fixed. Everything in Peirce's reality is in a state of constant fluctuation. Although at the scale of normal human perception many things look stable and constant, at the levels of our most precise measurements everything is fluid.

His attempts to explain the fluctuating nature of reality led him to another unusual conclusion. We are not passive observers of a reality that exists independently of our observation of it. Our observations shape reality. Reality to Peirce had to be experienced. There might be something that exists independently of experience, but whatever that is would not constitute reality.

Reality to Peirce could not be found in either the thing observed or the observer alone. Reality always emerges in the relationship between the observer and the observed. The observed influences the experience of the observer, and simultaneously the observer influences the reality of the thing observed.

Reality is not a static something that exists independently of us. Reality is an ongoing dance between us and the world. Neither we nor the world is ultimately real, only the dance is.

The reason we don't get the same measurement twice is because our previous measurements have affected the reality of what we are measuring. This is still a very odd idea for us today, but in the 1860s when Peirce started his musings it was even more unusual.

Peirce's philosophy was an inspiration to Werner Heisenberg, who was one of the architects of quantum theory and the founder of what is known as Heisenberg's uncertainty principle, which essentially says that because the act of measuring affects reality we can only be certain of one measurement at a time. If I measure one thing now, it will affect the thing that I measure, so I cannot be certain that any previous measurements still hold true.

Peirce never successfully completed his philosophical project. He was never able to fully redefine reality in this threefold way and describe to his own satisfaction the ceaseless interplay between experience, experiencer, and that which is experienced.

I believe the new paradigm will be built on this interactive and participatory view of reality. Reality will cease to be assumed to be a static background that holds true in all places at all times under all circumstances. Instead it will be seen as an ever-changing state of fluctuation that exists in the instant of being experienced before yielding unceremoniously to the reality of the next.

We don't perceive reality this way yet. Instead, we see a solid world with things moving on it like actors on a stage. As I have already stated, our consciousness is shaped by a things-in-space assumption in which the universe is a stationary background with things moving around in it. The things are where the action is. They compel us. We look at things, work with things, accumulate things, and love things. Things are material, that is, they matter. (Interesting to note that the word *matter* refers both to the physicality and the significance of things as if the two were inseparably linked.) Things are the stuff of life. We have been trained to pay attention to things. Things come in many forms. Money, jobs, people, feelings, birthdays, countries, and every hour of the day are all things. Everything and anything you can name is a thing. Things are the content of life, and we've been trained to value content. We are content junkies.

At the same time, we largely ignore context and take it for granted. The content of life is what matters; the context is just the bland background whose only function is to display all the wonderful things in front of it. Modern cosmology tells us that the ultimate context is the universe and the universe is an infinite expanse of empty space. If the ultimate context of life is nothing but empty space, then it's natural to think of it as largely inconsequential. In the new paradigm we will learn to be at least as attentive to context as we are to content, and this will change everything.

We give so much of our attention to things that we generally don't see them in context at all. We imagine that we just see things. We assume that the things we see are real. When we see a chair, we assume that there is something there to see. We also know that everything we see has qualities. Chairs can be big or small; they come in different colors, and they're made of different materials. Every chair we see is different, but they are all chairs. We relate to things like chairs as if all of their qualities have been painted on them. In the paradigm of things-in-space we have been trained to see things-with-qualities. What we might fail to recognize is that qualities don't just exist like paint on a house; qualities always exist in context, and that context shapes the quality of things and makes them what they are.

It was recently explained to me that it is a mistake to think of the characteristics of yin and yang from Chinese medicine as qualities that things have. Nothing is either yin or yang; things show up as yin or yang in relationship to the context that they appear in. The same thing will be yin against one background and yang against another. Saying something is yin is not a description of a quality of a thing. It is a description of the quality of a relationship between the thing and the background context that it is showing up in front of. The thing is not either yin or yang, but it can show up as either depending on the background.

And this is true of all of the qualities of life. Things don't have inherent qualities; they show up with qualities in relationship to the background they show up against. We are not separate from the background. Take a moment to look at the things around you now. Notice that you habitually see them as independently existing objects that have qualities belonging to themselves.

I'm sitting in a coffee shop, and I see a chair in front of me. From where I'm sitting I see it against a black background, and it looks very light. If I shift in my chair, I see it against a white background, and it looks dark. The quality of lightness or darkness does not belong to the chair. It is a quality that appears in relationship with the background it is viewed against.

We are taught to assume that the chair is the same and only its characteristics change. I want to ask you to experiment with the possibility that the chair you see against the black background is not the same chair as the one you see against the white background. I challenge you to say what exactly it is that stays the same if a thing's qualities change. What allows us to believe that things remain unchanged even when their qualities change? What is the thing underneath the qualities that doesn't change when the qualities do?

We are trained to assume that there is something really real underneath the appearance of things—and the appearance of things are not really real. We are taught that things exist independently of their qualities and characteristics, but it's hard to understand what it is that stays the same while all the qualities shift around. The German philosopher Immanuel Kant dealt with this by simply saying that the unchanging reality underneath all of the qualities is imperceptible to us, but he still assumed it was there.

Maybe there is another possibility to consider here; perhaps when something appears different it actually is different. Look around the room and shift your perspective and see how things change. I see the front of the person across the coffee shop from here. If I walk a few feet to the left, I start to see his back, and he becomes silhouetted in light. He looks different, and maybe he is different.

The qualities of the things around us are always shifting. We've been taught that these shifts in appearance are irrelevant to the reality of the thing itself. The thing is the same thing regardless of its qualities. We assume that things remain unchanged through all of the shifts in their characteristics.

If we let go of our attachment to the existence of the independently existing real things of the world, we might be able to change the way we see the world. Maybe things don't exist as permanent objects with qualities and characteristics smeared all over them. Maybe there are not things. Maybe there is just a field of relationships that we draw boundaries around to create the appearance of things.

Another way to understand the project of the American philosopher Charles Sanders Peirce is to see it as an attempt to describe all of reality based on the premise that reality can never be found in either content or context alone. Reality can only be found in the relationship between content and context. Look around the room again, and keep shifting lenses between seeing permanent independent objects that have qualities versus seeing a shifting field of relational qualities out of which boundaries are being drawn to create the illusion of things.

The static universe of things with qualities may start to feel dead to you. It just sits there while inconsequential qualities dance across it. On the other hand, the universe of relationship feels alive. Everything shows up fresh and new in every moment. Reality arises in the dance of foreground and background. This is the same dance that in Hindu philosophy is mythologized as the dance of the god Shiva and the goddess Shakti. Shiva is the background; Shakti is the foreground. And reality must have both. Yin only exists in relationship to yang. The world cannot exist without Shiva and Shakti. The world is not a thing that sits in empty space. The world is a dance of elements, some playing the role of content while others play context, and in the next moment everything can shift.

And you yourself are not a static thing that lives its life on the surface of an inconsequential stage. You do not exist as an object in the world; you are a dance of exchange that is evanescent and free. You are a life-form that emerges freshly in every moment of the dance. Each next step of the dance is shaped by the momentum of previous steps, but it is also shaped by the ever-new qualities of the world you are dancing in. You are moving and shifting in every moment, and the world is too. You are affecting the way the world shows up, and the world is affecting the way you show up. You are not the same person that you were a moment ago, and you won't be the same a moment from now.

It might be better not to even think of yourself as dancing because that can too easily be interpreted in terms of things-that-dance.

Maybe you are not a thing that dances with the world. Maybe you are the qualities that momentarily arise in the dance of the universe.

We have been exploring how a paradigm is an interpretive framework that shapes our reality by training us to interpret our experience in particular ways. The current paradigm has trained you to interpret yourself to be a material thing that exists in time and space. The illusion becomes complete once you become convinced that the fact that you experience yourself that way proves that it's true. In order to find your way out of this interpretation of yourself, all you need is an equally plausible alternative. We want to find an alternative belief that is as plausible as our current one so that we will be thrust into the uncertainty of not knowing how to determine which of them is true.

In the space of not knowing, which I earlier called "betweenness," the grip of the current paradigm releases, and we find ourselves free floating in a magical space between interpretations. At this point we don't know how to interpret our experience, and we become profoundly open and receptive to new possibilities. We have been calling this wormhole inquiry because it places us precariously at the edge of the current paradigm where we might fall into the experience of a new one.

In terms of our sense of self, all we need now is an equally plausible theory to the one that tells us we are a thinking-thing. As we already established, we have been trained to experience ourselves as a skin-encased being that experiences thoughts and feelings that are produced in our brain. In addition, the miraculous living machine that we are is believed to have been born into a universe of time and space that was here waiting for our arrival.

Just moments ago we introduced a poetic picture of ourselves as a dance, not a thing that dances, but the dance itself. This may feel aesthetically appealing, but I think that many of us will find it difficult to totally accept that description without a way of understanding it that will allow our minds to relax. I believe that William James came up with just such a way of understanding the world. In one of his famous essays he called it a "world of pure experience," and we are going to explore his conception here and see if it can help take us out of our thinking-thing sensibility into a new paradigm.

What if you are not a thing that thinks; what if you are more like an intelligent energy that is dispersed equally throughout the entire universe? What if everything you currently experience as reality is more like a movie projection? What if it all seems real, but it's ultimately only a projection? This of course was exactly the point of Plato's cave allegory.

From inside our current paradigm this sounds impossibly speculative. So let's take a moment for a wormhole inquiry. You can start by looking around you right now. What do you see? I see a table and a coffee cup. I pick up the coffee cup and feel the warmth of the ceramic on my skin. I put it down and hear the bang of the cup against the wood of the table.

Throughout this book we've been exploring how we are trained to see a world full of separate things when in fact it is more accurate to say that we are continually creating a world full of separate things by dividing up the dance of qualities of the sensational world into identifiable objects that we can label with words. I've just mentioned three of them: a cup, a table, and me. Of these three I have the distinction of being conscious, which means that I experience the cup and the table, but I don't imagine that they experience me. I feel the heat from the coffee on the outer edge of the cup, and I feel fully justified to assume the cup isn't being hurt by the high-temperature liquid it holds. I know what the table looks like, but the table has no idea that I'm here.

If I look at everything the way I've been trained to see it, then it all seems simple and obvious. I am a conscious being who is experiencing and manipulating a cup that sits on a table. The cup, the table, and I exist independently of each other. If I walk away, the table and cup will sit here until I come back. I am the living being in this scenario, and the cup and the table are inanimate objects. This is exactly the way we are taught to experience things, and as long as we do we can move smoothly through the current paradigm without much trouble.

Let's look again. Do you really see a table and a cup? Look at the cup closely. How do you know what you're seeing is a cup? How do you know it isn't part of the table it sits on? How do you know it's a three-dimensional object that you can lift up? Wouldn't you be surprised if you tried and it wouldn't budge? If you look closely, you will see that your perception of the cup is interpreted and constructed based on a host of ideas you have about what a cup is.

Let's keep looking. If I pick up the cup, how do I know that I am picking up a cup that is separate from me? We of course would say that's obvious. I just do it, and that's what happens. I reach out my hand, clasp my fingers around the handle, and use the muscles of my arm to lift it off the table. I don't have to prove that because it's obvious.

But questioning the obvious is exactly what we must do if we want to invoke a paradigm shift. So let's look past the obvious together. We need to look more deeply than the experience of picking up a cup because that experience is already laden with interpretation. Keep looking. If you pick up the cup slowly and really look at the raw uninterpreted data from your senses, what do you experience then?

I feel sensations that I assume are the muscles of my arm, hand, and fingers. I also see a collection of colors and shapes that I put together into a picture of a cup and a table. In the end what I actually experience is a collection of feelings, colors, and shapes that I use to construct an experience of me picking up a cup from a table.

So in fact it starts to look like even this little scene playing out in front of me is more a projection than a reality. This is exactly the realization that Immanuel Kant immortalized when he argued that we only ever experience a phenomenal reality that is constructed by our mind. Later William James dared us to recognize that we don't live in a reality of things at all; we live in a world that is created out of pure experience and raw sensation.

If you take some time with this wormhole inquiry and continue for an hour or two to pay attention to how your experience of everything is interpreted from raw sensation, something amazing starts to happen. The things that had seemed so solid start to feel more contingent and constructed. You feel less like you're moving around through space interacting with things separate from you and more and more like you are part of a creative process that brings the world into being freshly in each and every moment.

If you keep going, sooner or later you will begin to realize that you yourself are one of the phenomenal things that is being interpreted into existence. You are not a thing-in-space. You are an experience of being a thing-in-space that arises as part of the field of pure experience that reality is.

In the very first chapter of this book we stated that one of the most foundational assumptions of the paradigm that currently shapes our experience is the assumption of a division between subject and object. Now it is time to return to that foundational assumption, but having done so much work to dismantle many of our other deeply held assumptions we can explore it at a much more profound level.

In modern Western philosophy this split between perceiver and perceived was most famously articulated by René Descartes, and over the past few hundred years it has become embedded in our experience of everything. Which means that we experience everything as someone. Our experience of the world has become inextricably meshed with our experience of ourselves. We see a world of separate things of which we are one. We see ourselves as conscious things, and we see everything else as something that we are conscious of. We don't just experience things; we experience things as things that we are experiencing. In writing this I am attempting to bring to light a fact so close to us that it defies description. Those of us who endeavor to shift into a new paradigm must learn how to question this deeply. Again, this is what Whitehead was getting at when he wrote about analyzing the obvious.

What we've been exploring in this book is an experiential way to question the obvious by picking out an aspect of our experience that seems undeniably true and then asking if it really is. Right now I want us to question if we really are subjects experiencing objects. We start with what appears to be the obvious truth that we are all entities that perceive things in the world outside. For instance, I am sitting in my favorite coffee shop, and as I look around I see other people working on computers and talking together sipping coffee. I feel like a somebody that is seeing these people, and I have the distinct experience of being located over here looking out at them over there.

It is fairly easy to think in terms of a reality that is being shaped by a set of unconscious beliefs and assumptions. That doesn't challenge us too much because we can still feel like the self that is experiencing the reality that is being shaped. We can fairly readily imagine ourselves seeing the world through a lens of ideas that shapes what we experience.

I want us to go deeper than that by realizing that even the experience of yourself being a person who is experiencing the world through a paradigm is itself a projection of the existing paradigm à la Plato's shadows on a cave wall. When we think about the paradigm we are in, we are thinking about it through the paradigm itself. This puts us in the middle of a strange loop that places us in an unending cycle of having thoughts about a paradigm that happen inside the paradigm that those thoughts are about. What we are doing now is questioning our own existence. Are we really subjects perceiving objects? Effectively that means that I am asking myself if I exist, but the one who is asking the question is also the one whose existence is being called into question. This kind of circular questioning of the self has been used in esoteric spiritual traditions for thousands of years. As I mentioned earlier, it was famously utilized by the great twentieth-century Indian mystic Ramana Maharshi when he would instruct his students to contemplate the question, Who am I?

One of the most ubiquitous and insidious ways that our experience is shaped in the current paradigm is that it always includes the presumption of our own existence. No matter what we think, feel, or do, we assume that we are doing it. We generally never question whether or not it is really us that is having our experience. Think about how silly that last sentence even sounds—of course we are having our own experience. Who else would be having it? We have been deeply conditioned to believe that we are a someone (a subject) who is having an experience of something (an object), but is that necessarily true?

Take another look at the experience you are having right now. For me that means looking around this coffee shop again. Maybe noticing my feet on the floor, or the person standing outside the window.

What if there is no one having this experience? What if this is just an experience? What if part of the experience is seeing people in a coffee shop and another part is feeling like I am someone who is seeing people in a coffee shop? What if these two experiences, seeing the people in the coffee shop and feeling like the one who is seeing them, are just two different experiences that are coupled together out of habit? What if there is no one, no being or entity that is having either experience? What if reality is pure experience with no one behind it all having it?

You might protest. You might say it's obvious that I am having my own experience. Just look, everything I see, I see from inside this body. I can only see from over here where I sit. I can only feel my feet on the floor and not anyone else's. I see my inner thoughts and feelings, but I can only hear the spoken words of everyone else.

All of this seems to provide obvious and undeniable evidence that I am over here having my experience, and other people are over there having theirs. If you look at all the so-called evidence, you will start to find a mountain of assumptions underneath the obviousness of it all.

Why do I believe that feeling my feet on the floor means they are mine? Why do I believe that not feeling my neighbor's feet means they are not mine? Why do I believe that the thoughts I experience in my mind belong to me, and the ones being spoken through the mouths of others belong to them?

All of this evidence appears to lead unerringly to the obvious, undeniable, and inevitable conclusion that I am someone having my experience, and everyone else is someone having theirs. But—and this is the key—it is only obvious when looked at from inside the assumption of being the person looking.

From the vantage point of being a separate subject experiencing the world of objects, all of the experience we have points unerringly back to the obvious truth that we are a subject experiencing objects. They all repeatedly confirm that we are someone having an experience. But maybe that is only because our prior assumption has already shaped all of the experience into what we were expecting. We live in a self-shaping reality, and so we invariably find seemingly irrefutable evidence to confirm our prior assumption of being a separate entity looking out at the world.

So I ask you, what if there is no one having the experience you think you're having right now?

The liberating wormhole that we are dancing around when we ask this question is the insight that we might not exist. It is the startling recognition that the person that we thought we were—the one who answered to our name, made our choices, and felt our pain—was never actually here. Instead, there is just a field of pure experiences with no one solid underneath them all having them. It is a field of consciousness in which experiences and ideas about experiences keep unfolding. Some of those ideas are ideas about being someone, and those ideas give rise to the experience of being the person the ideas are about.

Our goal in this book was to learn about what it really takes to liberate the intelligent life force of the universe from our sense of self. That is the paradigm shift that I am interested in. The life force that animates your heart and mind is being squeezed through your belief in yourself. It comes through as your ideas, your feelings, and your actions, and those ideas, feelings, and actions can't expand beyond the limitations of being you unless you find a way to let go of who you think you are.

We've all heard stories about little old ladies who pick up two ton trucks to save a child. We've also heard about beginner's luck. And we've all probably experienced doing something that should not have been possible when the only explanation we can find for doing it is that we just didn't know that we shouldn't be able to.

I am trying to express something that is not so hard to explain, but impossible to understand. The person you are while you read these words and the person I am while I type them don't exist. That's it. That's what the whole book is about. We've been living in a story about characters that don't actually exist.

The living intelligence and energy of the life force of this universe wrote the book. But to do it, it first had to make up a set of ideas about a person called Jeff and then get all tangled up in them until the tangle of energized ideas about Jeff was able to write a book. To be able to understand what it had written, it needed to get tangled up in ideas about being you so that you could read the book. The life force that is reading this book through you is the same life force that wrote it through me.

We can relax into this possibility by letting go of the need to be the person we have historically been. Then we might see that the one who wanted spiritual freedom in the first place was never Jeff or you. The life force of the universe wanted spiritual freedom from Jeff and you. It wanted and still wants to liberate its potential from the limits of our ideas about who we think we are and what we think is possible.

Reality started as a singular conscious awareness. In that form it was wildly free and unconstrained by any distinctions or divisions. There were no parts and no separation. It was whole and unified and wonderful, but there was something missing. In this vast and expansive consciousness there was one thing that could not be experienced—relationship, connection, contact.

The longing for connection led the intelligence to seek out forms of self-identification that could hold awareness. Once they had stabilized, those platforms of identity could connect with each other. They could communicate and relate. They could fall in love; they could fight; they could have all the experiences that only arise in relationship.

Perhaps now is the time when the life force wants to reintroduce Oneness and unity into our paradigm of separation. Maybe what this is all about is the transformation of the possibilities of relationship by balancing the individuality and uniqueness that we have become so good at with the awareness of unity and oneness.

Of course, that is just a story about a possibility, but it seems to me that it is as valid as any other I've heard about the purpose of life.

WORMHOLE INQUIRY

In this inquiry I want you to occupy the space of the question, What if no one is having the experience I think I'm having? Just open into the space of possibility of that question and see what happens. Don't try to figure it out. Let the question work on you.

What if no one is reading these words? What if there is just an experience of reading words without anyone solid behind it having it?

What would it mean if we were to discover that we lived in a world of pure experience and that the person that we always thought we were having our experience never existed?

Let the question work on you. Just introduce it into consciousness and see what opens up. It might simply be a mysterious and intriguing sense of confusion. The question doesn't make sense. You don't know how to engage with it. Just stay with that feeling. Don't withdraw from whatever starts to open up. Allow yourself to drift toward the opening. If you get overly intellectual and try to figure out an answer, you will soon notice that the opening has vanished. If the opening disappears, all you have to do is return to the question. Let it open up again and find a way to move into the opening.

If there is no one having the experience that you are having, it means there is only an experience. That means that any experience we have of there being someone who is having an experience is itself just another experience. Everything I see, hear, taste, touch, or smell that might be me is just another experience. Any thoughts that I have and every emotion I feel are also experiences.

Keep looking at everything you can find around you and inside you. They are all experiences. Try to find something that is real and not just an experience. You can't. If no one is having the experience that you think you're having, it means that reality is made up of pure experience. Experience without an experiencer.

CHAPTER NINE
MORE THAN HUMAN

Throughout this book we've been challenging the assumption that a human being is an isolated vessel of consciousness. We are calling into question the seemingly obvious fact that we are beings with minds that generate thoughts and feelings. That is indeed the way it most readily appears to us, and yet when we look again we can see that it is just as reasonable to say that the universe itself and everything in it is giving off thoughts and feelings that we perceive with our minds. So why does it seem so obvious to us that we are consciousness beings in an unconscious universe? That is because we don't perceive the universe the way it is. We perceive a conceptual world that is shaped by our beliefs about it. We see ourselves as intelligent beings because that is what we believe we are.

When I say that we live in a conceptual world, what I mean is that we perceive concepts as much, if not more, than we perceive actual things. For example, I am sitting in a coffee shop writing. As I look around, I see tables and chairs, coffee cups and croissants, baristas and plants. I am not seeing objects; I am seeing concepts. The dog that just walked in with its owner does not see a barista behind the counter. They see an animal. They don't see a chair either; they see a thing. To see a chair, or a barista or a coffee cup, you have to know what one is. Most of the time we don't see objects; we see ideas about objects. We see concepts.

Our five senses make contact with the world. We perceive feelings, sounds, tastes, and scents. We don't perceive coffee cups or croissants. I perceive the coffee cup sitting on the table in front of me as a collection of sensations. I see redness and roundness; I feel smoothness; I smell bitterness. My mind takes these sensations and concludes that I am seeing a coffee cup.

Up until now it is very possible to read all that I have written and still be interpreting it from the vantage point of a separate self. You can imagine that you, the person you know yourself to be, are reading the thoughts of the universe, for instance. Now I want to take us someplace that is more difficult to comprehend because it necessitates that we move beyond the paradigm of a universe of empty space populated by mostly dead things and a few living ones. Where we will go now is into an experience of a living universe in which every part and every collection of parts is awake and aware. We are not intelligent living things that exist in a dead unconscious universe. We are part of a living universe, and our intelligence is an extension of the intelligence of the universe itself.

What makes this so difficult to imagine is that it can't be seen from a human perspective. To go this far out of the current paradigm we have to leave our species' point of view behind. The things-in-space paradigm, in which we have the distinction of being a thinking-thing, was conceived of from a human point of view. It is what human beings came up with after a few thousand years of looking out at the world and trying to explain what we saw. We did the best we could, and naturally the understanding we came up with reflected our own point of view. What else could we do? Our point of view was all we had to work with. And all in all, it doesn't seem so bad, except now that we've become such a global force it appears to be having catastrophic effects.

Let's slow down and review how we got here. The conceptual world of croissants and baristas that we were just talking about a moment ago is a second-order reality made up of a first-order reality that is itself made up of raw, uninterpreted sensations that we can call the sensational world. When we say that we live inside a paradigm, what we mean is that we live in a conceptual world that is defined and divided up according to specifically agreed upon lines of distinction. And the lines of distinction of our current paradigm were agreed upon because they were valuable to us.

The center of gravity of the current paradigm is the belief and experience that we are thinking-things. That means that I see myself as the dividing line that separates the world out there and the inner world of my thoughts and feelings. We see ourselves as things that contain thoughts and feelings. And we see the rest of the universe from the vantage point of assuming that we are the thinking-things in it. The paradigm that we are considering now is a paradigm of unity, oneness, or universal emergence. We introduced a metaphor to help us understand this strange new paradigm when we spoke about the North American beaver pond. In this chapter we will do our best to move beyond understanding a new paradigm into an actual experience of it.

Now we can return once again to the example of me typing this book. My fingers are gliding across this keypad tapping each next key in order to type words that match what I am thinking. Generally, we don't think of our fingers as intelligent. We don't imagine that our fingers know what we want to type and then do it for us. Even though it might look like they are acting with an intelligence of their own, we know that any intelligence they seem to be expressing comes from us. We know that we are the intelligent being that has fingers and that any intelligence the fingers seem to have is a reflection of ours.

But we don't hold this same view when we look out at the universe beyond us. When we imagine ourselves acting with seemingly independent intelligence, we assume that we are intelligent. This assumption subsequently necessitates that we create elaborate and sometimes bizarre religious and scientific theories to explain how a living intelligent being like us could ever have appeared in this dead and unconscious universe. Perhaps we need to reconsider. Maybe we are like the fingers of the universe expressing an intelligence that does not belong to us. Maybe our intelligence belongs to the universe as a whole.

If we think about the universe as a living being, we don't have the problem of wondering how life emerged from non-life. Instead we are seeing life evolve from one form to the next. It would also make sense that the characteristics and qualities of awareness would be different depending on the form of material that it was being expressed through. Every piece of matter is aware, but not all in the same way. A rock has awareness, but it doesn't have the same awareness that a dog has, and neither has the awareness of a sun.

What we are exploring is the possibility that we exist in a living universe where awareness is emanating out of everything. I am writing now in an airplane as I fly to lead a retreat. The chair I am sitting on is aware, and the plastic it is made from is aware; the wing is aware; the ground below is aware; every blade of grass down there is aware. Awareness is emanating out of everything, and all those different forms of awareness overlap and interpenetrate in ways I cannot imagine. The living universe is aware through everything in it. The view that I am describing here is similar to the one currently being explored by Dr. Timothy Morton of Rice University in his writings on the newly emerging philosophy of object oriented ontology.

It is time to consider what happens when awareness emerges through human beings. When the awareness emanating from a universal source passes through the human form, it has access to a distinct range of perceptual possibilities defined by the limitations of the human form. Of all the capacities that consciousness has in human form, one of the most extraordinary ones is the ability to identify things. We not only experience things; we identify them. We amalgamate sets of experienced qualities (what philosophers call qualia) into a single experienced thing that we label with a name. We conceptualize our experience and create things using language.

My experience of any identified conceptual thing is not an experience of something that exists separate from my identification/conceptualization of it. What I want us to consider is the possibility that conceptual things are real things with their own awareness. And of all of the things that we identify, there is one that is more primary than all the others. That thing is our own self. I identify myself as Jeff in the same way that I identify everything else, namely by taking a set of qualia and amalgamating it into a self-concept that I label Jeff. This identity is what I call my self, or my ego. We conceptualize ourselves, and that conception becomes a real thing with its own awareness. We conceive ourselves into existence.

What a magical image of reality we are exploring. Rather than empty space with some rocks in it, we see experienced conceptual things that continually come into being bursting into life and awakening into consciousness. Our consciousness and our capacity to generate conceptual things are continually creating new real things, new aware beings. One of those new aware beings is our own self. Human beings are magnificent creators. Just look around at everything that we have created. And yet we seem to have backed ourselves into a corner that we don't know how to get out of. Having imagined ourselves into existence we have gotten stuck in a rut.

Rather, we should say that the conscious awareness of the living universe has gotten itself into the rut of being human.

Returning to the model of reality that we explored in the very first chapter of this book, we will build an entire reality starting with nothing but a pure source of awareness that has nothing to be aware of yet. Then a process of creation occurs in which more and more forms are born. One of those forms, which called itself human, eventually became aware and then self-aware. As the universal awareness passed through this new self-aware human, it became identified as human and in so doing took on an identity that was much smaller than what it actually was. The universe forgot itself when it labeled itself as human, and it wedded itself to the range of perceptual possibilities that human beings have. I believe it is here that we can find the ultimate source, and the ultimate solution, to our global challenges.

Think about it. We've already talked about how we have created the world by drawing lines of distinction that divide our world into identifiable things and that those lines were drawn from our current human perspective according to the dictates of our own convenience. We created a conceptual world that was useful for us. This isn't anyone's fault. As an intelligent species, we inevitably conceptualized the world around us, and naturally we did so in terms that were aligned with our own needs. The problem isn't so much that we see a world that has been defined by our own needs. The problem is that we think we're seeing the world objectively when in fact we're not. So when we make decisions—even decisions that we think are good for the world—we find ourselves giving preferential treatment to the human world, often at the expense of other beings or even the world itself.

This is one way to understand how we have done so much damage to our physical planet. It's not that anyone wanted to harm the planet—no one ever would since we depend on it for the survival of ourselves and everyone we know. It's just that we went along year after year, decade after decade, century after century making decisions that were beneficial to the human world without realizing that this might not turn out so well for the planet. And even now that we recognize what we've done we find it difficult to stop the momentum of destruction. Before we can tackle a problem like global warming, we might first need to expand our awareness so that it can reach beyond the human conception of the world.

Here is an experiment that is easy to try. Go to a place you have been many times before and notice something you've never noticed before. I am in the same coffee shop that I have been in hundreds of times, and I never noticed that fire-alarm switch on the wall. I never needed one, so I never looked for one, and I never saw it. How many things are there in the world that as a species we don't have any need for, and so we don't even see? How much of the world is invisible to us because it isn't valuable to us? I believe that the global devastation of climate change is largely occurring because as a species we have such a profound impact on the world and our perception is filtered through a lens shaped largely by our own needs.

The question that we as a species must ask is this: Can we shift out of our profoundly human-centered paradigm and move into a conceptual world drawn from a vantage point that is not exclusively convenient to us? Can we move into a "more than human" perception of reality? How would we do this?

Many people are attempting to think on a global scale, but a shift in paradigm means more than thinking on a global scale. It is not enough to understand what is good for the world; we have to shift our experience of reality, not just our ideas about it. That means not only a cognitive shift but a shift in how our nervous systems present information to us. We need to move—mind, body, and spirit—into a new world and begin to perceive along lines drawn according to what is authentically good for the whole.

As we move beyond our currently human-dominated perspective, the world will change before our very eyes. It will open up to us in new ways. We will live in a different world because we will be experiencing differently. New options of response to our global situation will present themselves that simply do not exist in the world as we currently know it. In order to shift out of our human-centered worldview, we need to have some experience beyond it. Without at least a glimpse of another possibility it wouldn't even occur to us to search for an alternative to our current reality because, as I have previously discussed, reality by definition isn't supposed to be something that has an alternative.

Many people's initial experience of a different reality comes in the form of mystical revelation. As I said earlier, decades of spiritual practice have blessed me with a multitude of extraordinary experiences that have shifted my awareness beyond the familiar bounds of reality. These miraculous shifts in perception are journeys beyond the current conceptual paradigm into the non-conceptual experience of pure sensation. For times, sometimes brief, sometimes longer, I have lived in a dramatically different world. A world that is not shaped by the concepts that generally define reality. These experiences reside beyond our ability to understand or even remember clearly because the conceptual tools that we normally use to interpret our experience fail us. There are simply no words that can do justice to the new world we have been thrust into. Inevitably our attempts to describe these experiences fall far short of the majesty that we remember feeling when we were in them. Words are about as useful in capturing the fullness of spiritual revelation as a postcard is in capturing the experience of an exotic location.

Yet we are left with something—impressions that are less distinct but more compelling than normal memories. Having journeyed beyond the conceptual world of the human-centered perception of reality, we have seen firsthand that there are worlds beyond what we know. We recognize that the universe is bigger than the human mind can grasp.

We are also left with the distinct recognition that we are more than merely human in the way that we have learned to understand ourselves. The spaces we occupy in our revelatory experiences cannot be understood, and we cannot picture ourselves there, and yet in some uncanny way we know that we were there. It can be profoundly troubling to know something that you cannot understand or remember clearly. After all of the many experiences I've been blessed with, the one thing that I can conclude without doubt is that reality is bigger than I can imagine, and so am I.

In the midst of spiritual revelation the part of us that we know disappears. Our conceptualized self—our self-image—cannot exist in the non-conceptual realm of mystical revelation. Yet miraculously we discover that we can exist there, and the relief of being without the mirror of self-concept is one of the reasons why journeys into non-conceptual awareness feel so free. In these moments we also realize that our sense of self—the only thing we have known ourselves to be—is itself a product of the paradigm of human-centered conceptions. The person we thought we were is a projection of the same conceptualizing process that creates all of our experience, but, miraculously, we are more than that. Our journeys beyond the conceptualized world prove that there is much more possible for us and the world than we ever have, or even could, dream of.

What I am trying to express here is more challenging to grasp than you might be thinking. It isn't that hard to see that our perception of reality shapes reality, but I am saying something more than that. I am saying that there is no reality beyond our perception of reality. What we call real is a product of perception, and without perception it ceases to exist at all. We are not beings with the power to perceive reality. We are a perception of being a being with the power to perceive reality. Our perception of being human is not a perception of something that we are. It is a by-product of a perceptual process. Reality is a perceptual process, and part of what arises out of that process are perceptions of being individuals who perceive a real world outside of themselves.

Now take a moment to consider what I am saying. Notice yourself reading these words, and consider that the awareness that is reading them is not yours. Imagine that the awareness of the universal consciousness is passing through you and reading these words. And the unlimited source of awareness has gotten itself all tied up in being identified as you. The universe thinks that it is you reading these words. The universe thinks that it is me writing these words. The universal awareness, the vast consciousness that is the source of all life, currently thinks that it is us. The universe is stuck in the rut of being human. Can you allow yourself to feel this? Not just think about it, but actually feel the universe reading these words through you?

The journey of illumination in many mystical schools is a journey that moves our awareness from our identity as a self, or ego, into the universal source of awareness. Enlightenment experiences in these traditions are thought to bring us into contact with the original source of awareness prior to the shaping influence of identification or conceptualization. Before we are aware of identifiable things, we are just aware. This is what in some Buddhist philosophies is spoken about as pure awareness or pure experience.

I spent many years pursuing the experience of Universal Awareness and have been blessed with many dramatic experiences of it. These experiences are the source of my conviction that the universe is a living conscious being, but these experiences are only part of what is needed to re-create the world.

It is critical to realize that when we feel, when we think, and when we take action, we are not just doing those things; we are doing them as someone. Our feeling, thinking, and acting don't emerge out of thin air. They emerge out of an identity—out of a sense of self. Notice right now as you read these words that you are not just reading them; you are reading them as someone. If you feel into your experience, you will see that you are experiencing everything as someone. The awareness that is reading these words is passing through a sense of self, like water passing through a straw. If you let go of that identification, you will fall back into the ocean of universal awareness from which the water in the straw is being drawn. You will see that you are that ocean and always have been.

In our deep spiritual experiences we realize that we are not limited to the person we have always thought ourselves to be. We can move into Universal Awareness by untethering from our sense of identity.

The universe is alive and aware, and currently on this planet one of the forms it is emerging through is the human form. In our deep awakening moments we see for a few minutes, hours, or days that all is One, but those visions don't generally become permanent, because they are eventually usurped by the dominant paradigm of separation. The individual sense of self almost invariably claims these as experiences for itself, reducing them to memories of Unity and knowledge of Oneness.

Our current human form is not big enough to hold the unifying realization of Oneness. And the need for us to expand beyond the current human perspective could not be greater. The Universe we live in is not dead; it is alive; and we are it. Everything in the universe is infused with awareness because awareness is what everything emerges out of. The awareness that is reading this page is not originating inside you. It is the awareness of the universe in the form that our current human self allows it to take. That awareness has always had the potential to read, but the capacity to read only actualizes as it passes through you. This is how we become the vehicles through which the universe gains access to its own latent potentials.

New perceptual possibilities need to be explored. The current human self has reached the end of its capacity to cope effectively with the world it finds itself in. A new self will bring to light possibilities and capacities that we cannot yet imagine. We cannot construct this new self; we have to grow into it by detaching our awareness from our current sense of self and allowing that awareness to be available to be re-shaped into a new human form. In that form the awareness of the universe will see things that we cannot see, know things that we do not know, and do things that we could never do. This is the adventure of conscious evolution.

WORMHOLE INQUIRY

In this final inquiry I want to suggest that you re-read all or parts of this book from the point of view of universal consciousness. Don't read it as yourself; read it as the universe. How does the universe hear what is written differently than you do? What will the universe do with insights shared in these pages? How will this book help the universe remember itself and wake up from the dream of being you?

There is a second part to this inquiry that involves playing with pronouns. You will have to do this one the next time you are at a social gathering that gives you the opportunity to talk with a number of different people. As you speak to people, hear all of the pronouns that you use and all of the pronouns that you hear from others to refer not to the thinking-thing with a name, but to the universe itself.

When you speak to someone, wonder why the universe would want to say what you just said. When someone speaks to you, wonder what the universe is trying to tell you.

If you do this in the back of your mind for a while, you will start to experience every voice in the room, including yours, coming from the intelligence of the universe itself.

ABOUT THE AUTHOR

Jeff Carreira is a mystic, a spiritual guide, and a philosopher who teaches meditation and spiritual philosophy to a growing number of people throughout the world.

As a spiritual guide Jeff offers retreats and courses leading individuals from across the globe in a form of meditation called "The Practice of No Problem." Through this simple and effective meditation technique Jeff has led thousands of people in the journey beyond the confines of fear and self-concern into the expansive liberated awareness that is our true home.

As a philosopher Jeff is interested in defining a new way of being in the world that will move us from our current paradigm of separation and isolation into an emerging paradigm of unity and wholeness. He is exploring and teaching some of the most revolutionary ideas and systems of thought in the domains of spirituality, consciousness, and human development. He leads courses in this new understanding of reality and teaches people how to question their experience until previously held assumptions about the nature of reality fall away to create the space for a dramatically new understanding to emerge.

Jeff is passionate about philosophy because he is passionate about the power of ideas to shape how we perceive reality and how we live together. His enthusiasm for learning is infectious, and he enjoys addressing student groups and inspiring them to develop their own powers of inquiry.

In a world in which university education is often thought of as a vocational certificate, seeing someone obviously relishing the acquisition and sharing of knowledge for its own sake is inspiring.

—Dr. William O. Shropshire

Jeff has taught university students about Charles Darwin's influence on American thought, spoken with recovering alcoholics about the transformative philosophy of William James, and addressed Unitarian church groups about Ralph Waldo Emerson and the roots of their faith. He has taught college courses on philosophy, spoken at conferences, and led seminars worldwide.

Jeff is the author of six books. Three of these—*The Miracle of Meditation, The Practice of No Problem,* and *Embrace All That You Are*—clarify his teachings of meditation. The other three—*Philosophy Is Not a Luxury, Radical Inclusivity,* and *The Soul of a New Self*—offer a continuously expanding presentation of his revolutionary conception of reality and how it evolves.

For more information about Jeff or to book him for a speaking engagement, visit: www.jeffcarreira.com